advance copy of

Economic Stability is Attainable

*To the House of Lords
Library with the
Compliments of*

[signature]

25. 2. 75

*Any references to this work
should be prefaced by
the words "forthcoming book"
up until 1st April 1975.*

Economics

Empire Stocktaking (1930)
Empire Stocktaking (1932)
Agricultural Reconstruction (1933)*
Britons in Partnership (1933)
National Reserves for Safety and Stabilization (1939)
Commonwealth Stocktaking (1953)
Utilizing World Abundance (1958)
Australia in the 1960's (1961)
(*Preface by Sir Robert Menzies, KT, CH, when Prime Minister of Australia*)
A Firm Foundation for Economy (1962)
A Built-in Basic-Economy Stabilizer (1972)

And in lighter vein

The Adventures of a Jackeroo (1909)
The Romantic Story of Australia (1923)
(*Preface by Viscount Bruce of Melbourne, CH, MC, when Prime Minister of Australia*)
The Kangaroo Keeps on Talking (1924)
(*Introduction by Earl Baldwin of Bewdley, KG, when Prime Minister*)

*In collaboration with Henry Drummond-Wolff, MP

Economic Stability is Attainable

L. ST CLARE GRONDONA

With Prefaces by
Sir Roy Harrod, FBA
Professor Lord Kaldor
Lord Roberthall, KCMG, CB, and
Donald Tyerman

Hutchinson Benham, London

Hutchinson Benham Limited
3 Fitzroy Square, London W1

An Imprint of the Hutchinson Group

London Melbourne Sydney Auckland
Wellington Johannesburg Cape Town
and agencies throughout the world

First published 1975
© L. St Clare Grondona 1975

Set in Monotype Times
Printed in Great Britain by Flarepath Printers Ltd
St Albans, Herts, and bound by
Wm Brendon & Son Ltd, Tiptree, Essex

ISBN 0 09 123951 6

Forenote

This book incorporates, considerably elaborates upon and updates an Economic Research Council Paper *A Built-in Basic-Economy Stabilizer* prepared in late 1971 and published early in 1972.

Since then the blight of inflation has much worsened with essential commodity costs rising to absurd heights. But, if past experience be any guide, this unwonted stimulus will lead to primary producers so greatly increasing their outputs that, within the next couple of years, there could be such surpluses to (then) consumer-effective-demand as to cause prices of some commodities to fall – in some cases – almost as dramatically as they have risen.

The long-term objective of the system as described is to establish reserves of the widest practicable range of durable basics (without any forms of control or of coercion) so administered as to maintain market prices within prescribed, realistic levels of oscillations; *thereby ultimately to provide backing for currencies in terms of each essential commodity so held.*

Sponsorship

Although the basic raw materials for this Group of Companies are indigenous, we are sponsoring the speedy production of this book because we believe that, under the Grondona System, 'Economic Stability *is* Attainable' – by gradual process.

In short, we agree with the views of Sir Roy Harrod and the other eminent economists who strongly endorse his recommendation that HM Government loses no time in setting up a Special Committee with the terms of reference Sir Roy proposes in the last section of his Preface.

It would seem that, under the influence of this System, international monetary exchange would in due course become more stable than at any time since the abandonment of the gold standard – with its place being taken by essential durable commodities which are the real needs of men.

JOHN REISS *Chairman*
Associated Portland Cement Manufacturers Limited
Portland House, Stag Place
Westminster, London SW1   December 1974

The Back Cover

The excerpts from *Hansard* of 2.12.58 as printed on the back cover of this book are quoted in vindication of Sir Roy Harrod's statement in the second sentence of the opening paragraph of his Preface.

Mr Oram was later *Parliamentary Secretary for Overseas Development*, and the late W. T. Aitken was subsequently knighted. Mr Patrick Maitland is now the Earl of Lauderdale. Mr (now Sir John) Tilney was later *Joint Under-Secretary of State for Commonwealth Relations*.

Contents

Examples of fluctuations in prices of essential durable commodities having constant utility value

N.B. The run-back to the 1960s shows that such oscillations are no new phenomena. They have periodically recurred since 1920 – excluding only the period of war-time price-fixation accompanied by rationing.

Prices are per long ton to the end of 1972 and thereafter per tonne

SUGAR : Down to *£19.7* in 1962 – up to **£105** in 1963; down to *£12.3* in 1967 – up to **£32** within the same year; up to **£120** in 1973; above **£650** in November 1974, but fell to *£440* during December of that year.

COCOA : Down to *£94* in 1965 – up to **£434** in 1968; down to *£189* in 1971; up to **£970** in 1973 (July) and down to *£486* in November of the same year.

COPPER : Down to *£236* in 1964 – up to **£531** within the same year; down to *£331* in 1965; up to **£570**, again within the same year; down to *£430* in 1968 and up to **£818** (yet again, within the same year); down to *£414* in 1972 and up to **£1,085** in 1973 (November). During 1974 its price rose to **£1,400** in April but fell to *£564* in October.

LEAD : Down to *£50* in 1962 – up to **£155** in 1964; down to *£86* in 1971 and up to **£275** in 1973. During 1974 it ranged from **£324** in February down to *£217* in July.

ZINC : Down to *£63* in 1962 – up to **£140** in 1964; down to *£92* in 1966 – up to **£135** in 1969; down to *£114* in 1971 and up to **£760** in 1973 (December). During 1974 it ranged from **£875** in May down to *£319* in October.

8

Prefaces

By Sir Roy Harrod

Among those who have closely studied Mr L. St Clare Grondona's writings on commodity price stabilization he is widely regarded as the outstanding expert in this field. The tragedy of it is that his highly practical proposals have not long since been implemented. In this regard his foresight is exemplified in the extract from his 'Open Letter' to the Chancellor of the Exchequer in 1962 which appears in the first chapter of this work. Indeed, that prescience goes back more than fifty years when, in a book published in 1924, he first advocated the establishment of commodity reserves – specifically of wheat. To that work, the then Prime Minister (later Earl Baldwin of Bewdley) contributed an Introduction in which he wrote, 'The economic facts in his text may have more far-reaching effects than the author contemplates.' But nothing came of that.

When, in 1939, I agreed to contribute a Preface to his *National Reserves for Safety and Stabilization* I wrote: 'It is much to be hoped that the author's proposal will receive widespread and immediate attention. It has commendable breadth of scope and simplicity of outline. It deals with matters that are of urgent importance and proposes treatment on the scale worthy of the problems. But our leaders of late have shown a special aversion to such plans. They prefer niggling patchwork. It is a curious thing. They know that we are in difficulties; they profess an earnest wish to make our system work, preserving sufficient of what is tried and established for further developments to be orderly and controlled. Yet when a scheme is propounded for an orderly advance, they not unusually become quite shy and frightened and too often appear to be inhibited from giving it their consideration. May Mr Grondona's lucid advocacy of what is indeed an orderly advance, serve to galvanize them into action!'

That book certainly received widespread attention in the way of unequivocal commendation in the responsible Press. But the Govern-

9

ment of the day remained inert! Now again this nation stands in peril, mercifully not of war, but of economic disorder aggravated owing to our dependence for vitally essential needs upon external sources of supply.

His system, as now redefined and up-dated, proffers a long-term solution to a problem which, thus far, has baffled not only HM Government but governments the world over. It seems to me now to demand implementation, in which respect this Preface concludes with my specific recommendation which – as will be seen – is strongly endorsed at high levels among economists.

The violent oscillations in prices of essential commodities as listed on page 8 are patently chaotic. None would dispute the author's contention that it is impossible for a stable economic superstructure to be built upon such shifting sands. It is to rectify this disorder of affairs that he outlines a detailed practical remedy.

The keystone of the Grondona system is that, from the date of a Price Stabilizing Corporation's inauguration, it would ensure pre-specified minimum money values for every commodity brought within its scope; and he strongly recommends that the widest practicable range should be so included. Then, when this Corporation acquired reserves of any such commodity, currency would automatically be accorded both maximum *and* minimum values in terms of each so-held essential product. And that is a consummation devoutly to be wished!

The author has no illusions. As he emphasizes, because the malaise of inflation has progressively worsened over the years, its cure must be a gradual process. All he claims at this stage is that, under the influence of his system's standing ready to operate, there would be an immediate amelioration of present anxieties (vide paragraph A.12, Chapter 1); because the attainment of a firm foundation for the economy as a whole would then be seen to be in ultimate prospect – as a predictable pattern of cause and effect.

The rises in underlying total demand for basic commodities (or, in some cases, declines) usually proceed at a fairly regular rate. Oscillations in outputs of products subject to yield-variation, with resulting price-variation, point strongly to the need for a mechanism by which redundancies due to especially good seasons would be carried forward into lean years; but seasonal factors do not apply in respect of minerals which (in general terms) may be mined at will – at costs that depend on the location of ores and the metal-content of these. There is therefore no valid reason why market prices for metals should fluctuate as they do. If there were a sustained upward price movement due to constantly increasing demand with which supply was not able to keep pace, this *would* make sense. But, as brought to the surface in this work, great increases in market prices for many metals (as well as for various perennial increments from the soil) are usually followed by equally disconcerting market price declines – with a resulting disorder.

Price has various functions in the economic system. One is to be a signal to producers that more (or less) output is needed. On the other side a change of price, based on *lasting* supply conditions, may be a valuable signal to producers to make some substitution against or in favour of the product in question in their methods of production. Large oscillations in these prices destroy their power of being effective signals. Producers would clearly be wrong to make important changes on the occasion of a peak or trough price, such as they would make if the price level in question was likely to be permanent. But the oscillation gets in the way of a price signal performing the useful function it ought to fulfil. When there is a big ephemeral oscillation there may simultaneously be a genuine long-run movement upwards or downwards that it would be desirable for those concerned to take cognizance of. It becomes impossible for observers to disentangle any such genuine long-term movement from ephemeral oscillations. Thus they are left without the signals that they ought to have.

The oscillations do harm in other ways also. For instance, a movement may have a 'multiplier' effect on the economy of a country in which the commodity in question figures importantly; such multiplier effects may cause an economy to become overheated, or conversely.

From early times in the study of the business cycle an important causal role was assigned to primary product price fluctuation. Recently there has been some shift of emphasis away from the study of the business cycle. But it is still with us, and the orthodox methods of ironing it out have not proved to have been 100 per cent successful.

In an environment of continuing spiralling inflation, such as we have been having recently, commodity price oscillation can, as Grondona shows, have the effect of promoting the spiral. If the prices of some important basic materials rise, user industrialists may feel impelled, after a time-lag, to pass them into the prices of *their* products. But we do not necessarily get a reverse movement when the prices fall from supernormal levels, owing to uncertainties about

11

the future. A manufacturer is reluctant to reduce a quotation when he thinks that there is quite a good chance that he may have to put it up again. Consequent increases in the prices of finished products have further inflationary effects when spiralling is going on. They may cause wage demands to be greater than they would otherwise be, and this has a still further inflationary effect.

We are now especially interested in the affairs of the less developed countries. It is true that the sixties, christened ten years ago 'The Development Decade', have proved rather a flop in that respect. Nonetheless, interest in these countries must continue. Those importantly dependent on a particular primary product, or on a group of them, will be afflicted by strong oscillations in their domestic incomes and foreign exchange earnings. This is detrimental both to foreign investment in them and to their own forward planning.

The author deals with this matter in his Chapter 5.

The British scheme put forward during the war for preventing primary product price oscillation foundered partly because there was an influential element on the American side holding that these matters could best be settled by the mechanisms of the free market. There should be no conflict between the services that the free market mechanism can render and a scheme of the sort advocated in this book. There does seem to be some tendency to excessive oscillations in what are known in economics as 'perfect' markets. One may cite the Stock Exchange. In less than perfect markets in which suppliers make their own price quotations, the cost of production exerts a steadying influence. This anchorage need not prevent lively competition and meaningful price changes from time to time.

There have been 'perfect' markets in which official limits have been placed on price changes, and yet these markets have been very effective in balancing supply and demand. One such is the gold bullion market, another the foreign exchange market. In the latter case, there are fixed limits, but market forces play a very active part in balancing supply and demand within these limits. (Of course the limits proposed by Grondona would be much further apart; there would be a wider 'band' as it has been called.) There has been a movement of opinion recently towards having greater flexibility in foreign exchange markets. One plan is simply to have wider 'bands'. There is another plan, having a striking resemblance to the Grondona system, which is commonly called the 'crawling peg'. In this scheme free market forces would work in two ways. They would secure the balancing of supply and demand day by day within the statutory limits. But they would also be allowed to cause a gradual change in the exchange parity itself through time. Similarly under the Grondona system, while free market forces would govern supply and demand, a Price Stabilizing Corporation would always assure a known floor in the market for each commodity within its scope; and, *when any commodity was held in reserve,* a known market ceiling would likewise be assured – such floors and ceilings being predictably adjustable in conformity with pre-stated patterns of cause and effect. Nonetheless, within such limits (when both were effective) free market forces would continue to govern the long-run movement of any such commodity's price range itself.

I would call attention to two points about Grondona's work. One consists of its inherent quality of lucidity, precision, practicality, comprehensibility and, above all, simplicity. As the years have passed, he has introduced various refinements, to meet criticisms, and to deal with newly perceived difficulties. But these refinements have not tended to make his scheme more complicated; rather the other way round. A newly observed difficulty in his system as previously envisaged has suggested to him some change, not involving greater complication but simplification. This is evidence of a fine mind at work.

It happened to be my duty to attend the meetings of an interdepartmental committee which was framing a scheme for commodity buffer stocks, which I mentioned above, to be submitted to the joint meeting of Americans, Canadians and British in Washington in 1943. Sometimes the discussions in our interdepartmental committee got somewhat complex, and I recall thinking what a good thing it would be if we could have the clear brain of Grondona at work among us.

The second point I wish to refer to is that he has consistently believed that we, the British, can go it alone in setting up a scheme of world-wide ambit. This seemed a good deal more feasible before the war than, on first view, it appears now, but he has grappled with this point, and supplied figures to vindicate his contention.

After setting out his reasons for discounting the present practicability of internationally agreed inauguration and administration of his system, he shows in his Chapter 6 how each of a number of great commodity-importing nations could unilaterally adopt it in *principle* – without uniformity in the detailed functioning of each scheme, yet with all operating in harmony.

It is in this context that Mr Grondona makes brief references to some discussions he had with Mr Drugoslav Avramovic of the International Bank for Reconstruction and Development. I can testify that Mr Avramovic was deeply impressed by Grondona's magisterial grasp of the subject.

The following are some of the important features of the system as outlined in his book:

(a) No controls or regulations are involved.

(b) No preliminary international agreement has to be reached before its implementation by any great commodity-importing nation.

(c) Its successful functioning under any one such nation's auspices does not depend upon the good will of other nations.

(d) There is no element of exclusiveness about it, because – to the extent it was required to operate – the resulting advantages would be world-wide.

(e) Again to the extent to which it was required to operate, it would counteract inflation at the base of the most important sector of world economy.

(f) It would facilitate an expansion of well-founded (earned) liquidity.

(g) The necessary *investment* required would be moderate relative to the value of trade in commodities within its scope.

The world has been long-accustomed to Britain's setting patterns in political, legal, financial and social institutions that have served as models for emulation elsewhere – and London is still seen as a leading entrepôt for commodity-trading. Unilateral inauguration by this country of such a project as is advocated in this book would surely be one more step in keeping with our long tradition of institutional leadership in many fields of human endeavour – and thus regarded by other nations.

Earlier in this Preface I said the Grondona system seems to me now to demand implementation, but it would be perhaps too much to expect always over-burdened Cabinet Ministers to find the time necessary for that close study and thinking through of this proposal which is essential if its potential efficacy is to be made clear.

Therefore, as the issues involved are of transcending and urgent importance, I strongly recommend that, as soon as may be, HM Government should appoint a fully representative ad hoc Committee with terms of reference that would require it:

(i) fully to investigate the problem of serious instability in prices of durable essential commodities with resulting grave repercussions;

(ii) to take evidence in public and closely to scrutinize the Grondona proposal, and any other suggestions designed to rectify these economy-disrupting anomalies; and

(iii) to submit its Report and Recommendations to Cabinet with the utmost expedition.

If Mr Grondona were invited to appear before such a Committee fully to describe his project, answering questions as these arose, there could be little – if any – doubt that its findings would justify as worthwhile all the trouble he has taken in this field down through the decades. It has been said that the implementing of his system would mark the beginning of an era as surely as did the initiation of the gold standard, but without its fatal weaknesses. I believe that statement to be well warranted.

R. F. HARROD

By Professor Lord Kaldor

I have for many years supported the idea of stabilizing prices of basic commodities by means of international buffer stocks tied, if possible, to the creation of a new international currency. My ideas have been pretty close to those of Mr Grondona; the difference between us has mainly concerned the question of whether such an idea requires an international agreement among the leading importing countries for its implementation, or whether, as Mr Grondona supposes, it would be possible for a country such as the UK to initiate such a scheme through its own action, without waiting for others.

As I see it, the major attraction of a scheme of this kind, for which it would be difficult to find a substitute, is that it spreads the sources of 'money-making power' far and wide – among the commodity producers of the world – and would thereby tend to generate the maximum attainable rate of growth in world economy, and under conditions of stable prices, at least for basic materials. By ensuring that any increase in the output of basic commodities will generate a corresponding increase in the purchasing power of the producers, it will also ensure, through adequate 'multiplier' and 'accelerator' effects, that the growth of commodity absorption will proceed fast enough to match the long-term rate of growth of commodity production which, under the automatic functioning of the system, would gradually be brought into balance.

Those who object to schemes of this kind on the ground that they might generate too much money and too much income in the hands of the primary producers, and would therefore be 'inflationary' in their effects, fail in my view to understand the true nature of inflationary processes. These are to be found, as the experience of the last two years should have made evident, in a *shortage* of basic commodities relative to the need for them and not in any superabundance of such commodities. Inflationary pressures arise whenever the growth of demand for food and basic materials – which is governed by the *growth* of industrial activities – tends to outrun the growth of availabilities of such goods: the opposite case, when the growth of availabilities increases faster than demand (and which would require an acceleration of the growth of industrial production) is a cause of world-wide *deflationary* trends – as was shown by the experience of the years following 1929.

Mr Grondona's proposal would create a powerful automatic stabilizer for adjusting the growth of demand to the growth of supplies of primary products through its repercussions on the effective demand for industrial goods. When production exceeds consumption, world investment in commodity stocks would automatically rise: this would imply a supplement to incomes derived from current sales to consumers, and thereby stimulate the absorption of primary products through increased production and employment in the industrial regions. A shortage of commodities would cause a depletion of stocks; this would reduce producers' incomes relative to the consumers' outlay on such commodities; it would thereby reduce the effective demand for industrial goods until the excess demand for basic commodities was eliminated. Over a longer period it is of course quite inevitable that the flow of production and of consumption of basic commodities should be kept in balance, either through adjustments on the side of production, or of consumption, or both. Mr Grondona's scheme has the tremendous merit of making it possible for adjustments to proceed smoothly and continuously, without upheavals that now accompany this process; and it would do so by adjusting the rate of consumption to the limits set by production possibilities, and not the other way round.

In other words, in the longer run it is the supply of basic materials which would set the limit to the rate of growth of world industrial production and not, as now, the rate of growth of effective demand, emanating from the advanced countries, which governed the trend rate of growth of investment and production of primary commodities.

Looking at the matter from another angle, the Grondona system would enormously enhance the effectiveness of monetary policy. For the Central Banks of the world would then come to regulate the supply of money through open market operations in commodity markets (and thereby ensure that such operations have a *direct* and *powerful* effective demand and on incomes) and not in the market for high-grade substitutes for money (such as Treasury bills) the income effects of which are both slow and highly uncertain.

NICHOLAS KALDOR

By Lord Roberthall

Like Lord Kaldor, I have also been in favour of international buffer stocks as a means of price stabilization for many years: I had hoped that these would be established under the International Trade Organisation which was proposed at the end of the Second World War.

I therefore endorse the suggestion made by Sir Roy Harrod in his Preface that the Government should favourably consider setting up a Committee of Enquiry with terms of reference on the lines he proposes.

It is many years since Mr Grondona first discussed his proposals with me, and in the intervening period he has done a great deal to meet various criticisms which have been made. Meanwhile the problems caused by the fluctuations of commodity prices have not got any less. His perseverance should be a lesson to us all.

ROBERTHALL

By Mr Donald Tyerman

In 1939, while I was its Assistant Editor, *The Economist*, in reviewing Mr St Clare Grondona's book *National Reserves for Safety and Stabilization*, said: '*The author offers a plan of action to solve a problem which is peerless in its complexities and world importance*'.

The principles epitomized in this book are on all-fours with what Mr Grondona wrote in that book; and speaking quite personally

17

now – a generation later – I see no reason to differ from that opinion. Today, as Lord Kaldor recognizes, these ideas for effecting stabilization of basic commodity prices are powerfully connected with realistic plans for stabilizing currency exchanges. Indeed, the large and damaging movements in commodity prices, and the exchanges, in recent years underline these needs and their urgency as never before.

So I, too, readily endorse Sir Roy Harrod's recommendation in the final section of his Preface.

DONALD TYERMAN

Sir Roy Harrod, formerly Oxford University Lecturer in Economics, was Economic Adviser to the International Monetary Fund in the fifties. He was President of the Royal Economic Society (1962–64) and for some twenty years Joint Editor of The Economic Journal.

Lord Kaldor, Professor of Economics, Cambridge University, was Economic Adviser to the Chancellor of the Exchequer from 1964 until 1968.

Lord Roberthall was Director of the Economic Section of the Cabinet Office from 1947 until 1953 and, thereafter, Economic Adviser to HM Government until 1961.

Mr Tyerman was Assistant Editor of The Times *from 1944 until 1955, after which he returned to* The Economist *as its Editor for over ten years up to his retirement in 1965.*

N.B. *While both Lord Kaldor and Lord Roberthall (understandably) use the term 'buffer stocks', it is one that has been consistently avoided by the author for reasons given in paragraph B.21(c).*

The Theme

The superstructure of industry and commerce is built wholly upon primary products – basic food-stuffs and raw materials; and, as the costs of these – individually or as a whole – fluctuate unpredictably in an utterly senseless way, this superstructure is built upon shifting sands. Instability at its base inevitably extends upwards and is intensified throughout the whole economic and social edifice – not only nationally but internationally.

It is these shifting sands that must and *can* be buttressed to provide a firm foundation for national and for world economy. For too long have individual Governments sought unavailingly to establish internal stability in isolation – with no hope of success. For too long have there been equally unavailing strivings to achieve international agreement towards the same ends – decades of efforts that have proved as futile as attempts to mix oil with water.

The net result has been the blight of inflation – spiralling upwards and outwards from the base of economy – with money values internally (and externally in terms of exchange) going haywire. And in the background there looms the possibility – pessimists might say probability – of a complete breakdown of the (world) price structure as during the 'great depression' of the inter-war years.

This work shows how this seemingly intractable problem can be solved – not overnight but by a process which, though gradual, would nonetheless ultimately attain the desired results.

In short, what has proved impracticable by international action can be done *unilaterally* by any great *commodity-importing* nation not merely to the advantage of its own citizens but to that of all peoples. In this respect the United Kingdom, having to import some half of its requirements in food and over 80 per cent of its industrial raw materials, is an outstanding example.

If it be said that commodity price fluctuations reflect a pattern of cause and effect one is bound to agree, excepting as to the effects of the intrusion of the predatory speculator. It is therefore manifest that *it is the pattern of cause and effect that must be altered*; and that is the purpose of the price stabilizing system outlined in this book. Under its auspices there would always be known market floors for each of the widest practicable range of basic commodities, thus to engender unprecedented world-wide confidence among the producers concerned; and – but only in the fullness of time – there would be correspondingly ensured a market ceiling for each such product. Thereby, there would be established a known price range – or band – within which legitimate commercial enterprise *unfettered by any rules or regulations* would continue to have ample scope for lucrative dealings. In such a setting industrialists would come to be assured of continuity of supply (within each relevant price band) of their essential raw materials; and the disruptive element resulting from pure speculation would be eliminated.

What is most bewildering about the proposed system is its simplicity, an assertion which invites the question, 'Why therefore is it necessary to write a book about it?' The answer is that it must be made clear that:

(a) this project can be inaugurated and become effective without any financial leap in the dark;

(b) the maximum investment involved could not exceed a pre-scribed relatively negligible sum for the establishment of commodity reserves which would ultimately provide backing in real terms not only for sterling but for all currencies;

(c) this system's administration would provide no scope whatso-ever for the bureaucrat; and

(d) far from becoming a charge on public funds the probability is that it would become something more than self-supporting.

No attempt is made in this work to suggest a solution in respect of the salary-and-wage factors involved in any form of production or of service. However it will be conceded that the most powerful element in support of demands for recurring increases in remuneration is that engendered by rises in the cost of living. If such costs – especially of essential foods and clothing – can be stabilized (if not reduced) under the proposed system's aegis the solution of that problem will be to that extent facilitated.

All that is asked of the reader at this juncture is that he endeavour to put into limbo his preconceived ideas, if these appear initially to conflict with the proposals that follow – and that he read and think through this work with an open mind.

'What is a £ Sterling?'

Prior to World War I, Bank of England notes carried a PROMISE TO PAY ON DEMAND their face value in gold coinage. In August 1914, these were replaced by *Treasury Notes* inscribed thus: *Currency Notes are Legal Tender for the Payment of any Amount, J. S. Bradbury, Permanent Secretary, HM Treasury.*

In 1928, Bank of England notes again appeared, then (and still) inscribed (e.g.) thus: *I Promise to pay the Bearer on Demand the sum of One Pound,* followed by the Signature of the *Chief Cashier.*

That such a *Promise* means no more than that one piece of paper can be exchanged *on Demand* for another piece of paper carrying the same inscription does not seem to disturb anyone.

Mr Bradbury became Lord Bradbury in 1925. Shortly before his death in 1953, *The Times* published this letter from that former Permanent Secretary to HM Treasury:

> SIR, – I have often been asked 'What is a £ sterling?' and, finding my inability to answer that question rather humiliating, I addressed it in turn to many of my friends who might know. The best reply I was able to get is that it is 'A Promise by the Chief Cashier at the Bank of England to Pay, at some date which Parliament may hereinafter determine, whatever Parliament in its wisdom may direct him to pay'.
>
> No doubt that is satisfactory as far as it goes; but it does not go very far. After all, what the man in the street wants is neither a bit of gold nor a promise to pay an abstraction; but something he can exchange for a loaf – or forty loaves – of bread, and maybe for a few fishes.
>
> Your obedient servant,
> BRADBURY.

This caused no more than a ripple of amused interest. But the disturbing fact is that there is no real measure-of-money-value in

Britain or anywhere else – which is one root cause of recurring economic disorders.

What – likewise – is a US dollar, a deutschmark, a French franc, or a yen? If that question were put to the Finance Ministers concerned their answers would inevitably be as vague as Lord Bradbury's. And that unsatisfactory disorder of affairs must continue until every unit of currency has known maximum and minimum exchange values in terms of basic goods essential to human well-being. In short, all the evidence goes to show that *monetary reform is not attainable by agreement* as to any one nation's paper currency's exchange values in terms of other nation's currencies – because there is no common denominator to which to relate these.

In physical spheres we have measures for length, breadth, volume, weight, density – and so on – which have enabled men to go far in mastering matter. In contrast, *because of the absence of money-value-measures*, economics (in many respects) is a pseudo-science – something of patches, of expediency, and of compromise in which all-too-fallible human judgement essays to do its best – too often contriving to do its worst.

NEED FOR CONFIDENCE-ENGENDERING CURRENCY

The real worth of any currency is its exchange value in terms of essential goods and of essential services – both of which factors are inevitably governed by the immutable law of supply and *effective* demand.

Essential goods in their original basic forms are in two broad categories: those which are durable in that they can be held in reserve at low cost for protracted periods without appreciable (if any) deterioration; and those which are perishable – unless of types that can be preserved by artificial means.

It is with durable commodities that, at this stage, the system advocated in this work is exclusively concerned: industrial metals, textile and fibrous raw materials, natural rubber and various chemical – and other – basics, as well as grains, pulse and certain other foods and animal-feeding-stuffs – all in primary form. *It is upon continuity of supply of these that man's well-being depends.* Many of them are naturally durable and – subject to the inexpensive precautions indicated in Chapter 3 – all can be held in reserve for long periods without adverse effects upon their utility.

The first and incontestably attainable objective is to accord to (relevant) *primary producers* (the world over) positive assurances that a known minimum price (a product's 'low *point*') is obtainable for every exported unit of their output – with productions beyond commercial market absorption (at or above the relevant low *point* levels) being saleable to a Price Stabilizing Corporation, something which – as will be shown – can be achieved at surprisingly low investment-cost.

The second – but *conditional* – objective is similarly to accord, to (relevant) *user-buyers*, assurances that the cost to them of every unit of their requirements, *if such commodity(ies) be then in Corporation reserve*, shall not exceed a known maximum level (a commodity's 'HIGH *point*').

THE ORIGINAL GOLD STANDARD

(a) Gold is the only commodity ever to have had its price held stable for a long period when, for some 80 years up to August 1914, the Bank of England *valorized* this metal by standing ready to buy it at 77s 9d per standard ounce, and to sell it at 77s 10½d – here termed the *gold points*.*

A sovereign weighed a quarter of an ounce of which 99.765% was 'fine' gold and the rest of hardening metallic blend. A Bank of England note could always be exchanged (prior to August 1914) for its face value in gold coinage.

(b) Other external-trading nations followed that example, each *unilaterally* establishing its own *gold points* in terms of its own currency; and, thereby, prior to World War I, because the currencies of all participating nations had known values in terms of gold and, as things that are equal to the same thing are equal to one another, there was stability in foreign exchange.

That gold is not essential to man or beast is not at issue.

(c) While the Gold Standard was never internationally administered – much less so controlled – its automatic multinational functioning facilitated international trade; but it did *nothing* towards stabilizing prices of essential commodities.

*In practice, the Bank of England took account of such factors as freight and insurance. As will be shown in what follows, commodity-points under the system as described in this book would invariably be related to (preceding annual average) import costs *inclusive* of freights and insurance.

RESERVES VITAL FOR ANY FORM OF PRICE STABILITY

The effectiveness of the Gold Standard (in stabilizing currency exchange *in terms of that metal*) was wholly dependent on each participating nation's having reserves of this ('universally' accepted) token of wealth because, while any nation's low *gold point* (its buying prices in terms of its own currency) could be constantly maintained, its HIGH *gold point* (its selling price in its own currency) was effective only when it held gold in reserve.

CURRENCIES BACKED BY DURABLE ESSENTIAL COMMODITIES – THE ATTAINABLE GOAL

It is by an application of the *principles* of the 'gold points' system, but with an elimination of its rigidity and detailed administration, that the system advocated in this work deals. It shows how, by *gradual* process, sterling (and other currencies) would come to be backed by the widest practicable range of durable, essential commodities which are the prime needs of mankind.

Author's Precis of Commodity Price Stabilizing System

OBJECTIVES: Realistically to stabilize prices of durable essential basic commodities, thereby ultimately to accord to currencies a corresponding stability in terms of each such commodity.

i. The proposals in this work do not constitute a plan as with 'A Five-Year Plan'. Rather do they describe in detail a constantly-operative system leading to the establishment of reserves of imported basic commodities so administered as to stabilize their prices within predictable, relatively narrow ranges of market fluctuations without any interference with normal marketing processes. Under such auspices (and only under such auspices) will it be possible *for producers*, whether operating in primary fields or engaged in manufacturing, *to make their own plans*, and with a measure of confidence which (thus far) has been conspicuous by its absence.

ii. While, as will be shown, this system could be inaugurated by any great commodity-importing nation, it has always been the author's hope that the United Kingdom will take the initiative, thereby setting a pattern in this vitally important matter.

iii. Therefore, let it be assumed that a British Price Stabilizing Corporation (PSC) be presently Statutorily established, financed by HM Treasury within precisely predictable limits (as made clear in B.3 of Chapter 2), and as aloof as is the Judiciary from political, departmental or any other sort of influence or interference.

iv. PSC's functioning is designed ultimately to bring about realistic stabilization of prices for each of the widest practicable range of imported essential, durable, basic commodities that have constant utility-value, in place of the fantastic fluctuations (brought to the surface on the page facing the opening of Sir Roy Harrod's

25

Preface) which recurringly disrupt our whole economy – nationally and internationally.

v. While the attainment of this system's objectives must be a gradual process, abnormally high prices (such as those obtaining in the latter half of 1973 and in 1974 and if past experience be any guide) so stimulate greater production of the affected commodities that (sooner or later) outputs of these so increase as greatly to exceed then current effective demand, and their prices decline steeply – with other unfortunate repercussions engendered by the thus reduced reciprocal buying-power of the basic producers concerned.

vi. So accustomed had people become to this disorder of affairs that, many years back, economists coined a term 'the trade cycle' which came to be accepted as something inevitable. It is long-over-time for this bogey to be exorcized, not by recourse to 'bell, book and candle' but by the application of the principles of simple logic. The potentials for increased outputs in all forms of essential basics are dealt with in Chapter 5.

vii. To illustrate (in principle) the proposed workings of the anomaly-rectifying system described in this work, let 'X' represent any one durable commodity within PSC's scope – whether a basic food-stuff, feeding-stuff or industrial raw material.

viii. (a) Commodity 'X' is accorded an initial Valorizing Index (the Index) *based upon* (though not necessarily at par with) the average of its import costs per ton or other standard unit during a prescribed period of (say) five years immediately preceding PSC's inception.

(b) PSC then stands ready to buy 'X' at (say) 10 per cent below such Index – which is 'X''s (initial) low *point* – subject to satisfactory pre-appraisal at profferer's cost and to his delivery in prescribed substantial units-of-volume (or in multiples thereof) to the appro-priate of PSC's reception depots; and, thereafter, for as long as any part of so-acquired reserves are held, PSC will sell on demand to collecting buyers, but only at the same percentage *above* Index which is 'X''s (initial) HIGH *point* (*effective only when PSC holds reserves of 'X'*).

N.B. Obviously the average cif price over the preceding quinquennium might prove too low to be set as the *initial* Index in view of the extent of the general inflation that had occurred, especially during 1973/74. Hence the initial level of such Index might need to be weighted in proportion to the extent to which overall inflation obtained as at date of a British PSC's inauguration (*vis-à-vis* the then immediately-preceding quinquennial average of cif prices).

Conversely, if deflation happened to be rampant at date of this system's inauguration the *initial* Index might need to be somewhat below the immediately-preceding quinquennial average of cif prices.

ix. Under PSC auspices there is *always a floor in the market* for substantial dealings (in every commodity within PSC's scope) at close to whatever is the then low *point*; and, when reserves are held, there is a ceiling in the market for substantial dealings at close to the level of the then HIGH *point*.

x. While PSC imposes no time-limit as to the applicability of 'X''s *initial* Index and *points*, its functioning conforms to a pre-stated pattern of cause and effect – as follows: An accumulation in PSC's holdings equivalent to (say) one-tenth of preceding annual average volume of imports of 'X' – termed a BLOCK – causes the values of its Index and *points* to fall automatically by (say) 5 per cent; and, if a second BLOCK of 'X' so accumulates, there is a further fall of 5 per cent (of *initial* levels); as there is if and when any additional BLOCK (of the same commodity) so accumulates.

xi. This process reverses automatically if, after having accumulated reserves in excess of any first BLOCK (or maybe of more than two BLOCKS) of any one commodity, PSC's holdings of that product diminish – BLOCK by BLOCK – as a result of its being required to sell. Thereby, its functioning conforms realistically to the law of supply and demand – considered over the long term.

xii. In the event of PSC's not acquiring holdings of this or that commodity within its scope after a prescribed period (perhaps of a year or maybe two years) following its inception, there is a provision under which the Index for that product rises automatically by (say) 5 per cent – or more or less – annually until PSC does acquire stocks thereof; whereupon the then Index becomes that commodity's *initial* Index – see Chapter 2 (B.7).

xiii. PSC, *per se* inert, never *enters* markets. It is not actuated by the profit motive although, to the extent to which it was required to operate as a seller, it could hardly fail to be financially self-supporting – if not to be a substantial premium-earner. *All the initiative to cause it to function must come initially* from sellers of their own volition; and, *later, from willing buyers.* It is in no sense coercive in that it has no power – nor implied authority – to impose any sorts of controls or regulations on the trading community. In contrast, however, its own functioning is subject to arbitrarily rigid regulations of which all are made aware from the outset (vide Chapter 3).

N.B. In the event of this Corporation's accumulating what would ordinarily be termed 'profits', that is, after its (always low) administrative costs are met, it is suggested that all such accrued premiums should be held in a Special Suspense Account for use as the nucleus of what might be termed a 'Disaster Relief Fund' to be available for release in appropriate circumstances – a matter elaborated upon in Chapter 6 (F.13).

xiv. PSC buys and sells *without national discrimination* – solely on the merits of each commodity. It pays for its purchases in sterling, and *accepts only sterling when selling.* While there is a proviso that, in certain circumstances, PSC's payments for any commodity might be deferred for intakes beyond certain pre-specified large accumulations of any one commodity, this would occur only in the highly improbable event of a direct instruction from the Chancellor of the Exchequer – vide B.10. Operating (or standing ready to operate) strictly in accord with the principles enshrined in this system, PSC's functioning is not hampered (in respect of commodities with which it is concerned) by such impediments as tariffs – or the like – with which commercial trading has (increasingly) to cope; because *all its transactions in commodities on which duties or other charges are levied are under Customs and Excise Bond.*

xv.   There is nothing of the Star Chamber about PSC's functioning. It regularly publicizes its holdings (if any) of each commodity within its scope – with day-to-day holdings immediately ascertainable on telex enquiry. Such information would, of course, be of the utmost value to all primary producers and all user-industrialists involved. Obviously the extent to which PSC would be required to buy (and later to sell) this or that commodity is an open question. But, always in the background and always ensuring market-floors for all the products with which it was concerned, its constant readiness to operate would be an unprecedented steadying influence on all relevant market dealings.

xvi.   Political considerations or other factors subject to frequent change do not enter into the philosophy on which this system has been devised – based as it is on pure physical economics. It could be aptly said to have had its origin in Genesis, when Pharaoh's dream as interpreted by Joseph led to the establishment of huge reserves during the seven years of plenty to provide for the Egyptians in the succeeding seven years of famine.

xvii.   From the date of its inception, the MAXIMUM value of a currency in terms of every commodity within PSC's scope is *that* money's purchasing power at the level of *that* product's low *point*; and, when any commodity is held in PSC's reserve, the *MINIMUM* value of the same currency is its purchasing power at the level of that commodity's (then effective) HIGH *point*. This is elaborated upon in Chapter 2 read in conjunction with Chapter 6 treating of that *multi*national (as distinct from international) adoption of this system – which would probably follow in due course.

xviii.   It is not practicable for this system to be inaugurated internationally, nor will it ever be in the absence of an international currency.

xix.   In contrast, it is reiterated, any great *commodity-importing* nation (of which the United Kingdom is an outstanding example) can establish its own Price Stabilizing Corporation – operating exclusively in its own currency. This is fully explained in Chapter 6 wherein it is shown that, while no preliminary agreement is essential, a measure of concord in principle (as in F.4) would be highly desirable. In the event all such individual national PSCs would ultimately achieve harmonious relationships – by operating according to similar patterns of cause and effect. Let it suffice here to point to the fact that, when effective, *the Gold Standard was never internationally administered*. Rather was it multi-nationally adopted (after the United Kingdom had set the example) when – despite all its shortcomings – it at least harmonized international trade to the extent of stabilizing currency-exchange. *But it did nothing* towards stabilizing the prices of the real needs of men.

xx. The better working of existing commodity agreements as between producers and consumers in groups of nations (and the negotiation of further such agreements) would be greatly facilitated under this system's auspices – a matter dealt with in Chapter 7.

xxi. A most important feature of this system is that PSC will accept lodgements in its custody of commodities owned commercially (either by producer-sellers, intermediaries or user-industrialists) against which it would issue its *Warrants* which, subject to essential conditions, would be firm securities for bank loans (vide Chapter 2 **(B.14)**).

xxii. This short precis, while indicating the innate simplicity of this system, provokes so many questions that the full text needs to be studied if (a) the economic practicability and the small amount of Governmental investment potentially involved, and (b) the simplicity of its non-bureaucratic administration, are to be made clear.

xxiii. It is suggested therefore that the reader refrain from forming any conclusions regarding the proposals in this work after reading merely this brief epitome.

A BRITISH PSC *vis-à-vis* THE EEC

An obvious question arising is whether or not the United Kingdom's Membership of the European Economic Community could preclude Britain's taking unilateral action in initiating the proposed system. This matter is dealt with in Chapter 1 (A.15).

1. In Retrospect – and Potential Prospect

A.1   THE WORSE OF TWO BANES.   The bane of world economy in the 1970s is inflation whereas, in the twenties and much of the thirties, it was *deflation* – of which two maladies deflation was infinitely the worse as those who lived through the 'great depression' can testify.

A.2   THE ATTAINABLE GOAL.   The theoretical maxim: '*If prices are to remain unchanged, every increase in the volume of trade needs to be matched by an increase in the amount of circulating money – and vice versa*' is just not on, as successive Chancellors of the Exchequer (and their opposite numbers in other nations) are well aware. However, it *is* within the scope of practical economics to apply that maxim – within predictable limits and with a reasonable prospect of success – to all durable primary commodities such as metals, textile raw materials, rubber, grains and certain other food-basics, as well as to many animal feeding-stuffs essential to the production of meats and other ordinarily perishable foods; in short, to most of the primary commodities on which the superstructure of industry and commerce is built.

A.3   ECONOMIC ISOLATION IMPRACTICABLE.
(a) It is here germane to quote from an 'Open Letter' I addressed (in August 1962) to the then Chancellor of the Exchequer – Mr Reginald Maudling – which prefaced a short book devoted to the same theme as that now dealt with in this work. That excerpt read:

> The economic problems confronting any British Government are not confined to the United Kingdom. They extend – in less or greater degrees – to all the countries of the free

world. In short, Britain's own economy cannot be dealt with or controlled in isolation – to the extent of making it reasonably stable. If HMG is to establish a firmly based economy it must be by a means of which the rest of the world (tariff barriers notwithstanding) can take equal advantage – with the long-term effect being a firm foundation for *world* economy and with no excluding of the countries of the Communist bloc.

The system I propose could gradually provide standards of money-value (within predetermined relatively narrow limits) in terms of those forms of real wealth which are basic essential commodities. That goal cannot be achieved overnight. In the nature of things the process must be slow. But, in the long term, it can become effective to the great good not only of the people of the British Isles and of the Commonwealth (in the wording of the once much-vaunted *Atlantic Charter*) of 'all the men in all the lands'.

(b) After a lapse of thirteen years, it must be said that the attainment of the goal at which the functioning of the system I advocate is aimed would now take longer – perhaps very much longer – than if it had been statutorily inaugurated in (say) 1965 (or much earlier, following a specific presentation of my proposals to Sir Stafford Cripps as Chancellor of the Exchequer in 1948!).

A.4 ENGENDERING CONFIDENCE. However, what *could* be achieved expeditiously would be to engender that measure of well-founded confidence (in place of current disruptive misgivings) which would follow an announcement by HM Government that it had decided to put this proposed system into effect as soon as might be – to be in readiness to operate according to a prescribed pattern of cause and effect.

A.5 FLUCTUATIONS UNBRIDLED.
(a) On the page opposite the opening of Sir Roy Harrod's Preface are a few examples – of the many that could be cited – of fluctuations in prices of essential durable commodities which show the extent to which the superstructure is built upon shifting sands. *It is these that must be buttressed.*

(b) The attainable objective of the system described in detail in this book is to *give money predictable values*, within predetermined narrow ranges of price oscillations, *in terms of such commodities* – thus to provide a firm foundation for the economic edifice as a whole – both nationally and internationally.

(c) Sugar was no sweeter at £105 a ton in late 1963 than at under £13 in 1967, nor at £650, to which it rose in late November 1974, only to fall to £440 within the following month. Cocoa was no less nutritious at £94 a ton in 1965 than at £171 within the same year; nor when its price soared to £970 a ton in July 1973 – as compared with £288 a mere four months earlier. Copper had no greater utility value at £818 a ton during 1968 than it had had at £256 in 1964; and *its* prices ranged from £454 up to £839 within the first nine months of 1973; and to £1,400 in April 1974 – only to fall to £564 in December 1974. Such oscillations do not make sense by any reckoning; they are wholly economy-bedevilling.

(d) Later in the text the stabilizing influence on the price of each of these (and many other) commodities, if a British Price Stabilizing Corporation (PSC) had stood ready to function at the beginning of 1965, will be made clear. However, to indicate the potential effectiveness of this system it may be as well to mention here how the prices of sugar would have fared if a PSC had stood ready to operate as from 1 January 1965 – along the lines briefly summarized in the *Precis* on pages 25–30. The following are the factors relevant to the functioning of PSC in relation to that product.

> Over the preceding five years (1960–1964 inclusive) the annual average imports of sugar had been 2,360,000 tons at an average cost (cif) of £45 a ton. This taken (illustratively) as the *initial* sugar Index would have resulted in an *initial* low *point* (Index *minus* 10 per cent) at £40.5; and a (conditional) HIGH *point* (Index *plus* 10 per cent) at £49.5.*

A.6   WHAT MIGHT HAVE BEEN.   In the event, with no PSC to stop the rot, the price of sugar (which, as already mentioned, had been up to £105 in October 1963) ranged during 1965

---

*That the situation in respect of sugar is currently highly complicated by various factors (dealt with in Chapter 7) does not affect the validity of this illustration in principle.

from a maximum of £24.5 down to £17.7. It may suffice here to say that if PSC had stood ready in 1965 to buy at the *initial* low *point* of £40.5, it would obviously have accumulated huge reserves of this essential commodity; and so long as any part of such reserves were held, the maximum price for sugar could not have risen above the effective HIGH *point* of £49.5 a ton.

A.7 FACTORS INFLUENCING MARKETS.
(a) In the absence of any effective price stabilizing authority, when prices are on the decline (a buyers' market) many user-industrialists are inclined to suspend buying – or much to reduce the volumes of their purchases – maybe because they then hold substantial stocks, or, more likely, because their competitors – by holding back for longer periods – may buy more advantageously; and this *per se* tends to increase the rate of price decline. Conversely, in a rising (sellers') market, there may be a rush by user-industrialists to buy (especially if their stocks are low) lest – by holding back for a period – they may have to pay very much higher prices.

(b) It is in such circumstances that the outside-speculator (with no interest whatsoever in the use of the product as such) enters the field. More will be said about him later. Of course there is the technique of 'buying forward', the success of which requires highly specialized knowledge and acumen – in the absence of which it sometimes happens that the forward buyer later has cause almost to wish he had died when he had had the measles – as witness the loss by a certain eminent firm in 1973 of £32½ million in respect of cocoa forward buying. All manner of facts and rumours as to conditions in commodity-exporting countries: political discords, industrial unrest in the way of strikes or strike-threats, lockouts or lockout-threats, adverse weather conditions or forecasts, unexpected releases from strategic stockpiles (to which the US Government is prone) – the factors, real or fictitious, are legion – affect what is termed market sensitivity.

A.8 BASIC PRODUCERS' REACTIONS.
(a) Unusually high prices, whether or not there are actual shortages – then or in prospect – stimulate widespread in-

creases in production which, in turn, tend to lead to surpluses to *then* current needs, and prices fall accordingly. Seasonal factors apart, perennial increments from the soil can be increased more or less at will. But whereas outputs of such products as grains and sugar-beet can be greatly increased within a single season, several years must elapse before there can be greater outputs resulting from expansions in plantation and pastoral enterprises.

(b) As to industrial metals, when prices are unduly low, outputs of ores can be reduced – but with two unfortunate results because (i) this causes unemployment among miners (e.g., when outputs were cut by 50 per cent from certain African copper mines during the earlier sixties); and (ii) it increases whatever are then the output costs relative to constant overheads and to the servicing of the capital investment involved.

A.9 THE INFLATIONARY SPIRAL. Inordinately high prices for essential primary commodities engender inflation (more money for less goods) at the base of economy because such changes in money values *in terms of essential basics* extend upwards – gathering momentum the while – throughout the whole economic edifice. In short, when costs of basics soar, and remain abnormally high for somewhat protracted periods, it is inevitable that the selling prices of the finished products – be these processed foods (e.g., bread-stuffs are processed wheat) or other consumer-needs – likewise rise, not only owing to the greater cost of the relevant raw products but because increases in living-costs necessitate higher wages and salaries in all sections of secondary, tertiary and servicing enterprises. It is thus that inflation – having commenced at the base – gathers that self-generating momentum with which we are all too familiar.

A.10 UPWARD MOVEMENT OF DEFLATION AT BASE OF ECONOMY SEVERELY RESTRICTED. In contrast, when *deflation* (less money for more commodities) occurs at the base of economy – even if prices for primary durable products fall far below actual production costs – this does not likewise extend upwards because it seldom leads to any appreciable reduction in the selling price of the consumer-product – for understandable reasons. The purchase by processors and manufacturers of basics is always itself a gamble; and, though their raw-material costs may fall steeply during a few months, these user-industrialists have no assurance whatsoever that there will not again be considerable price advances in terms of basic commodities due to one unexpected cause or another; and their first concern is for their own shareholders. In any event, however steep be a fall in raw-material costs, they have had to continue to pay *at least* the same wages and other expenses. So it is that the self-actuating up-going spiral of inflation continues – with constant aggravations due, not only to progressively increasing wages and salaries, but also to the activities of predatory speculators in both commodities and currencies. (One is not moralizing in so saying, because it is perhaps true to add that most of us would engage in such quick-buck-making activities if we had the wherewithal and astuteness!) The real menace here is not a small investor who may devote £100 or so to a commodity-gamble, but already very rich individuals or companies whose activities are absolutely ruthless. The extent of such operations is made evident in Chapter 4 (D.5, D.6).

A.11 PAST UNEQUIVOCAL ENDORSEMENTS OF PROPOSED SYSTEM. (a) While it is almost proverbial that the individual given to saying (after the event) 'I told you so!' is highly aggravating, it is with all-too-much justification that I happen to be in that category. Following the appearance of my first book (on this theme) *National Reserves for Safety and Stabilization, The Times* published a leading article in unequivocal support of the proposals it contained. The following are excerpts from that Editorial:

... The benefit to both primary producers, and to trade and industry generally would be incalculable, since output programmes could be planned without the risk that violent fluctuations might upset the soundest and most conservative of plans. Almost the only person to suffer would be the predatory speculator, generally an outsider and not a regular dealer. . . . This work should be taken in hand now when everyone is animated by a common purpose. . . . There could be no more effective reply to gibes about pluto-democracy than to show by practical action of this kind, that democracy is capable of reconciling the claims of individual and national liberty with those of economic security.

That book was equally well received in all sections of the responsible Press including *The Economist* which concluded its review thus:

The scheme would require the fixing, not of prices but of a reasonable range of movements of prices. It has been very fully thought out (with a very shrewd perception of the criticisms that might be levelled against it) and it offers a plan of action to solve a problem which is peerless in its complexities and world importance.

(b) The proposals in that work, published as far back as 1939, were on all-fours (in principle) with my subsequent writings – with details in elaboration – on this subject; and the same may be said of what appears in this book, with the workings (or, as I now term them, the gearings) of the system I propose being adjusted (illustratively) to the general economic situation in 1975.

A.12 ESSENTIAL ASSURANCES TO PRODUCERS. The immediate effect of the establishment of a Price Stabilizing Corporation would be to engender an unprecedented measure of confidence among producers of every commodity within its scope – *and the wider the range of these the better* – because they could then plan their production programmes in the knowledge that there were known floors in all relevant markets at the level of each product's 'low *point*' and that such floors could not alter excepting in precisely predictable circumstances; and then by only minute percentages which would effectively prevent anything remotely approaching the frustrating, irrational fluctuations which theretofore had been their banes. Of course, as is made evident in the foregoing but is here repeated, it would be only if and when PSC came to hold reserves of any commodity – acquired at the behest of sellers not able to secure commercial prices at (or above) PSC's buying price – that there would be a market ceiling (at the level at which PSC would sell on demand – a product's 'HIGH *point*') for each commodity then in its reserve.

A.13 INVESTMENT FINANCE INVOLVED.
(a) The means by which PSC's operations would be financed, which are fully explained in Chapter 2, will show that the *cash investment* to which it would be potentially committed

during the initial three years of its functioning in respect of a range of commodities the preceding annual import cost (cif) of which had aggregated £1,000 million, *would not exceed £90 million*; or *pro rata* if the preceding annual average cost of all commodities within PSC's scope had been greater (which it probably would be) or less.

(b) In the text which follows (B.4) it will be fully explained how (and why) the margin between the low and HIGH *points* is constantly equivalent to 22.2 per cent of the low *point*; whereby (when the HIGH *point* is effective) that is the percentage range in which bargaining can take place between commercial sellers and buyers. However, while this *percentage* margin is constant, the margins *in terms of money* become progressively less after the intake of the first BLOCK (one-tenth by volume of preceding annual average imports) and at the intake (if any) of each additional BLOCK.

A.14 FURTHER UNEQUIVOCAL ENDORSEMENTS. It would seem apposite here to quote excerpts from highly perceptive Editorials dealing with my book *Utilizing World Abundance* (published 1958) in *The Director* (Journal of the British Institute of Directors), *The Manager* (Journal – as then titled – of the British Institute of Management) and – by way of contrast – *Tribune*. The reason these journals are quoted at such length is because what they say *needs* to be said; and because they carry a degree of conviction that no author could achieve by extolling (what he believed to be) the merits of his own proposals!

THE DIRECTOR: Mr St Clare Grondona boldly outlines a programme for tackling one of the root causes of booms and slumps: the violent ups and downs in prices of primary products. . . . For the producer of basic materials, uncertainty about prices overshadows all plans on which more efficient production would depend. For the customer there is the problem of unpredictable costs of materials which frustrates intelligent budgeting and choice of materials and imparts a de-stabilizing palsy to the flow of trade and international payments.

One of the worries troubling the world today is the effect of the slump in commodities upon the entire course of the free world's economy. In the past, piecemeal, private schemes for 'orderly marketing' of basic materials almost always led to restriction of supply. When prices were stabilized, they finished up too high. It is to this vital problem that Mr Grondona proposes a detailed practical solution. . . . It is a brave attempt to cure one of the most glaring maladies of the free world economy; and, at the same time, to anchor our own currency to goods with a true and lasting value. (February 1958.)

(Perhaps someone will convey the substance of the latter part of the immediately foregoing sentence to those high authorities who are – and who have for so long been – wrestling unsuccessfully with the problem of effecting monetary reform.)

In a further Editorial in January 1960:
Since *The Director* welcomed Mr Grondona's proposals in February, 1958, his scheme for moderating swings in commodity prices has been widely and variously praised as an economic masterpiece, sensible, simple and business-like. The author has addressed MPs, won supporters in all three Parties, and had his proposals pressed on the Government in parliamentary debate. As an author, he could hardly expect more laurels, but as an ardent reformer he must be disappointed by the failure of the Government to betray any indication of having studied his imaginative yet highly practical programme. One explanation could be that Ministers have not fully studied its detailed provisions for varying prices according to stocks held and for deferred payments in prescribed circumstances. Only slightly less flattering is the alternative explanation that the Cabinet have no time to bother with measures of reform that are not backed by any specific lobby of producers or other powerful interests. By avoiding any favours to sectional interest, eschewing subsidies, and promising fair play to producers, users and final consumers of raw materials, Mr Grondona's system was not calculated to appeal to party political expediency. It has been said that 'everybody's business is nobody's business', but what are governments for if not to serve general, as opposed to sectional, interests? . . . For all its rigorous detail [this is] a straightforward and appealing project.

THE MANAGER: . . . It can be only a question of time before man's reason and self-interest overcome his inertia and Mr St Clare Grondona's proposals are accepted. When they are they will define the beginning of an era as surely as did the introduction of the gold standard (but without its fatal weakness). He shows how an economy based on manufacturing and depending on imported basic products may overcome its apparent helplessness – and, to boot, how the problem of currency exchange rates may be solved. The desirability of such a system will not be questioned by any manufacturer or economist, least of all if he is British. . . . That Mr Grondona's scheme is not international, but either national or multi-national, is its greatest merit. No international agreement has to be reached, no other country's good faith relied on. It is in Britain's interest to introduce it on her own. If other countries follow – as it would be in their interest to – so much the better. . . . His system would stabilize commodity prices; improve our balance of payments; reduce long-term inflation; do much to prevent slump; safeguard British investments abroad; and afford . . . the best possible compromise between completely free exchanges and the so-called fixed exchanges that, in practice, are subject to unpredictable devaluations (and the fear of them). . . . We may have to wait long for a time as propitious as the present for this system's inauguration. (March 1958.)

TRIBUNE: The devastatingly simple scheme in *Utilizing World Abundance* is so attractive . . . and the benefits for its operation could be so great that it ought to be promptly taken off the drawing-board and sent to the workshop – in this case the Commons. (24.1.58.)

In the seventeen years that have since elapsed, the forebodings so specifically expressed in *The Director* have all-too-unfortunately materialized (again and again), most dramatically during 1974.

In that interim what is virtually a new generation has taken over, and I can only hope that effective heed will now be paid to what appears in this book.

A.15 UNILATERAL BRITISH ACTION *vis-à-vis* THE EEC. Without doubt the question will be raised as to whether the United Kingdom's Membership of the European Economic Community would conflict in any way with a decision by HM Government to establish a British Price Stabilizing Corporation to operate as proposed. The answer is an emphatic 'No!' – if due credence be accorded Governmental assurances that the real sovereignty of individual nations comprising that Community is unaffected. In this connexion it is essential to keep in mind that it would be a *sine qua non* that all PSC's transactions in commodities that are subject to either nationally-imposed or *EEC-imposed* duties or excise would be under Customs and Excise Bond (vide B.9).

A.16 PROSPECTS FOR AN EEC PRICE STABILIZING CORPORATION. At time of writing it is an open question, to be answered by the British Electorate, as to whether or not the United Kingdom is to remain within the EEC; and the Electorate's answer will doubtless be influenced by the outcome of current re-negotiations of the terms on which the Heath Government joined the Community at the beginning of 1973. Of course, it would be ideal if there were established an EEC Price Stabilizing Corporation – but that would not be a practical proposition until and unless there was a common currency throughout that Community; and that prospect appears somewhat remote. However, there would seem to be every good reason to expect each of the major commodity-importing nations comprising the EEC to establish its own stabilizing corporation. And that is something that could lead to a considerable degree of harmony in counteracting those nefarious influences which thus far hamper external basic producers on the one hand and, on the other, user-industrialists within the EEC. This matter is elaborated upon in Chapter 6.

2. A British Price Stabilizing Corporation

B.1 BRITISH INITIATIVE ASSUMED. Let it be assumed that there is statutorily established by HM Government in the United Kingdom a Commodities Price Stabilizing Corporation (PSC) financed by the Treasury, and administered by a small Board responsible thereto, to have within its range essential imported durable basic commodities the average cost (cif) of which over a stated period of immediately-preceding years had not exceeded a prescribed amount here termed the *Key Control Figure*.

Objectives:

(a) by gradual process (without PSC's entering competitive markets and without any form of coercion) to acquire reserves of such commodities;

(b) to administer so-acquired reserves in such a manner as to keep market prices for such products within predictable relatively narrow ranges of fluctuations; and thus

(c) *to provide currency-backing at maximum and minimum levels in terms of each so-held commodity.*

B.2 WITH KEY CONTROL ILLUSTRATIVELY AT £1,000 MILLION. (a) It is imperative that the implementing of this system should not involve any possible financial leap-in-the-dark. Hence, the potential maximum investment commitment (however unlikely to be reached) must be made clear from the outset. In order to simplify how this can be achieved let it be supposed that the prescribed period of preceding years was set at five years, e.g., 1970 to 1974 inclusive, with the assumption that the average annual aggregate import costs of the commodities to be brought within PSC's scope had been £1,000 million, only because this is a convenient figure on which to base illustrative workings. That sum in fact went near to covering the annual average costs of wheat, maize, soya bean, sugar, cocoa and coffee; wool, cotton, jute and other fibres; copper, lead, zinc and tin; and rubber – during the quinquennium 1969–73. However, if a wider range of commodities were brought within PSC's scope, the Key Control would need to be correspondingly higher – something elaborated upon in Chapter 4 (D.3.)

(b) On the £1,000 million illustrative basis, and assuming the system to be geared and financed as illustrated in this book, the maximum cash-investment to which PSC could be conditionally committed could be set at £90 million (i.e., 9 per cent of the Key Control) during the three years immediately following its inception. If PSC's investment-outlay were subject to any greater (or less) Key Control, its cash-investment during the initial three years would be *pro rata* at 9 per cent of whatever Key Control had been determined by Statute. Thus, if this had been set at £2,000 million, which it might need to be having regard to what is in the 'N.B.' following Paragraph viii of the Author's Precis, and especially if a much wider range of basics such as pig-iron, ferrous ore, raw materials for the chemical and fertilizer industries, timber and wood pulp were included – which would be highly desirable – the then maximum cash-investment possible during the initial triennium would become £180 million (i.e. 9 per cent of £2,000 million). In the event it might prove that £1,500 million would be a more than adequate figure.

Subject to what is in the intervening text, the validity of that statement will be made clear in paragraph B.10 of this Chapter.

B.3 INITIAL VALORIZING INDEX AND COMMODITY POINTS. (a) PSC's functioning requires that there shall be determined for each commodity within its scope what is here termed an *initial* Valorizing Index (the Index) *automatically* and *predictably* adjustable in prenotified circumstances related to each product. It would be on this Index that each commodity's *points* – PSC's buying and (conditional) selling prices – would be based. The low *point* at which PSC would stand ready to buy, at seller's behest and subject to rigid conditions, would be at a prescribed percentage *below* Index; and the HIGH *point*, at which (when it held reserves acquired at the low *point*) it would sell on demand, would be at the same percentage *above* Index.

The conditions governing PSC's purchasing would require satisfactory pre-appraisal *at vendor's cost*, with delivery – likewise at his cost – in prescribed-size units-of-volume, as in Chapter 3 (C.3) captioned 'Transactional Procedures'. And its sales would be in the same units-of-volume which buyers would themselves have to collect.

As made evident in Chapter 3, the administrative financing of PSC would be such as to avoid (as far as possible) its being committed to any imponderable expenditures – of which transport and handling costs of commodities are typical examples.

(b) While PSC's functioning could be geared in many ways it is of fundamental importance that, once such gearing had been initially determined and publicized, it should not be altered in any respect excepting by Statute; and then only after a prescribed period of (it is suggested) at least two years in respect of annual cultivations (products sown and harvested within single years); and appropriately longer for any other types of commodities – depending on the periods elapsing between initial investment-outlay and the stage at which resulting increased output begins.

(c) Although the gearing as described in what follows is primarily illustrative, it would seem likely to prove satisfactory to those directly involved – basic producers, intermediaries and user-industrialists; and it should certainly be to the advantage of the public as a whole. However, *special regard must be paid to what is in paragraph B.24 in this connection.*

B.4 HOW GEARING WOULD GOVERN PSC'S FUNCTIONING. (a) Let 'X' represent any one commodity (or any special type thereof normally marketed as such) within PSC's scope; and, to simplify an explanation of PSC's functioning in conformity with the (long-term) law of supply and demand, suppose the average annual import cost (cif) of 'X' (plus any allowance made to compensate for inflation – again having in mind the 'N.B.' after paragraph viii (b) of Author's Precis) had been £100 per ton*; and that this was adopted as 'X''s *initial* Index – with its (initial) low *point* at 10 per cent *below* Index (£90) at which PSC would stand ready to buy; and with its *conditional* (initial) HIGH *point* at 10 per cent *above* Index (£110) at which (when it held reserves of 'X' acquired at the low *point*) PSC would sell on demand.

(b) With the *points* always at 10 per cent below and above Index, the margin between low and HIGH *points* is a constant 22.2 per cent of the low *point*, e.g., the difference of £20 (between £110 and £90) is 22.2 per cent of £90; and that percentage-margin obtains at whatever level the *initial* (or subsequently adjusted) Index stands. The reasons for taking a five-year annual average of costs at British port of entry (and not an average of market prices) as the basis of the *initial* Index are fully explained in Chapter 8 (H.1).

B.5   PREDICTABLE INDEX-AND-POINTS ADJUSTMENTS – A 'BLOCK' DEFINED. The *initial* Index and *points* would remain at their original levels unless and until there had accumulated reserves of 'X' equivalent to (say) one-tenth of the average annual volume of this commodity as imported over the prescribed period of years preceding PSC's inception – such one-tenth aggregate being termed a BLOCK.

Thus, if the average imported volume of 'X' had been 500,000 tons, one BLOCK of that commodity would be 50,000 tons – to have acquired which at £90 a ton PSC would have made a cash investment of £4½ million. From the date of its first intake – and for as long as any reserves of 'X' were so held – PSC would sell on demand to collecting buyers at £110 per ton which (apart from handling charges for which PSC would not be responsible and brokerage) would *then* represent 'X''s market ceiling – at least for dealing in the prescribed units-of-volume.

*Thus – merely for illustration – if the actual average cost cif of 'X' had been £90 per ton it might be deemed necessary to add (say) £10 to that figure as an off-set to then inflation, thereby bringing the *initial* Index up to £100 per ton.

45

B.6 CONDITIONAL AUTOMATIC INDEX-ADJUSTMENTS. If and immediately a *first* BLOCK of 'X' had been taken into PSC's reserve, the Index-and-*points* level (of this commodity only) would fall by (say) 5 per cent, *and* by precisely that (or other prescribed) percentage of their *initial* levels at the intake (if any) of each subsequent additional BLOCK of 'X' – with automatic adjustments as tabulated below in the extremely unlikely event of reserves of anything approaching such tonnages accumulating. The word 'conditional' appears under 'HIGH' *point* because it is effective only when PSC comes to hold reserves; and it ceases to be effective if such reserves become exhausted.

Blocks	Tons (cumulative)	Index per ton	Low point per ton	High point per ton
1st	50,000	£100	£90	£110 (conditional)
2nd	100,000	£95	£85.5	£104.5 (effective)
3rd	150,000	£90	£81.0	£99.0 (effective)
4th	200,000	£85	£76.5	£93.5 (effective)
5th	250,000	£80	£72.0	£88.0 (effective)

And so on.

N.B. This process reverses automatically if PSC's holdings diminish BLOCK by BLOCK, up to the *initial* levels, but no higher excepting as shown in the following paragraph. That in certain circumstances (of which all concerned would be aware in advance) payments by PSC for purchases in excess of a first BLOCK of any commodity *might* be deferred is fully explained in paragraph B.10.

B.7 CONDITIONAL *Raising* OF INITIAL INDEX AND POINTS (a) If a prescribed period (say two years or less or more) elapses without its acquiring reserves of 'X' (i.e., of any commodity within its scope) the Index and *points* for that commodity shall rise automatically by (say) 5 per cent or other prescribed percentage (of the original *initial* levels); and by a further such percentage after each subsequent twelve-months until the date on which PSC does acquire reserves of 'X', whereupon the then Index and *points* shall become its new *initial* Index and *points* – with conditional adjustments as in the preceding paragraph.

(b) Such raising of *initial* Index shall likewise occur if, following disposals by PSC of reserves previously acquired of 'X', PSC has not held any replacement of such stocks for two years – or for whatever be the prescribed period.

This provision is to ensure that ultimately PSC will acquire reserves of the widest practicable range of basics within its scope – each then a currency-backing.

(c) The potential in the way of vast increases in world productivity of most of the essential commodities, even of wasting assets such as minerals for many decades to come, and certainly of perennial increments from the soil, is dealt with in Chapter 5.

B.8 ESTABLISHING RELATIVITY OF VALUES. The provision for possible raising of the *initial* Index is designed to adapt automatically to overall inflation so long as this malaise continues. Fundamentally, however, it is not the price (or cost) in money terms of any individual item of essential merchandise or of any essential service as rendered – *considered in isolation* – which is of significance. It is in fact the relativity of values (or costs) of each of all forms of essential merchandise and of each form of essential service which matters. To suggest that all such relativities of values could ever be satisfactorily achieved would be to suggest the unattainable. But it is certainly feasible to aim at the clouds with a good prospect of hitting the treetops. Thus, while we may dismiss the likelihood of attaining the ideal of an all-round-relativity of costs, it is demonstrably practicable ultimately to establish cost-relativity for basic commodities, in realistic terms, within predictable narrow ranges of price fluctuations via the automatic functioning of this system.

B.9 NO NATIONAL DISCRIMINATION – ALL TRANSACTIONS IN STERLING AND UNDER *Customs Bond* IF APPLICABLE. PSC would buy (and later sell) without national or other sort of discrimination – solely on a commodity's merits. It would pay for its purchases in sterling, and *would accept only sterling when selling*; and, where applicable, *its transactions would be under Customs and Excise Bond.* Thereby PSC's operations would not be restricted by tariffs; and external producers would have access to sterling (i.e., to reciprocal buying power) not only from their commercial sales (on which duties had to be paid) but also from disposals to PSC on which no duties would be levied – at that stage. Thus would entrepôt trading be facilitated (as in B.17).

B.10 POSSIBLE BUT *Improbable* DEFERMENT OF PSC'S PAYMENTS. (a) If and immediately a first BLOCK of 'X' had been taken into PSC's reserve – and for so long as a first BLOCK remained intact – PSC's payments for further purchases of *that* product *might* be deferred (but only on the very improbable specific direction of the Chancellor of the Exchequer) for three years, taking the form of Three-Year Bonds carrying interest of (say) 10 per cent – not compounded. These Bonds would be strictly non-negotiable in the commercial sense; but they could be transferred to the Treasury of the *country of origin* of the commodity (in deferred payment for which any had been issued) in exchange for that country's domestic currency, if *that* Treasury so approved and on such terms as it decided.

> N.B. If the willingness of vendors to accept such Bonds be questioned the reply is that the choice would be theirs alone. The alternative would be to sell on the market for what such offerings would fetch in cash. Some might do this – but the more prudent would doubtless realize that such action would be extremely imprudent.

(b) In the event, it is his own nation's currency which is a producer's prime need. Assuming his country's Treasury to have approved his request, it would then be holding a short-term British-Treasury-Guaranteed security which, on redemption, would carry a premium of 30 per cent. It might well be that (by special agreement between the Bond-holding Treasury and HM Chancellor of the Exchequer) credits so acquired could be used in advance of redemption date. If, for example, Bond-holding nation 'A' had outstanding debts in the United Kingdom, the Chancellor might approve of PSC Bonds being used in reduction of such debts; or some other special circumstances might obtain which would influence him to approve of earlier than Three-Year redemption; e.g., if the bi-lateral balance with nation 'A' were in the UK's favour.

> N.B. It is to be admitted that there might be some doubts (in the minds of those proffered Three-Year Bonds) as to

the comparative value of sterling (*vis-à-vis* other major nations' currencies) as at date of Bond redemption; because it might be that, when redemption of such Bonds became due some time during the fourth (or subsequent) year following PSC's inception, sterling's external value had depreciated in terms of (say) US dollars (if the continuity of value of *these* were accepted, as a criterion – as they had been over a period of years) either by deliberate devaluation – or for some other reason. Hence, to engender complete confidence in the estimation of actual (or potential) Bond-holders, HM Treasury might *guarantee* that it would adjust any such deficiency (the measure of which might be determined by some such impartial authority as the International Bank for Reconstruction and Development) by adding to the amount due on redemption the precise sum in sterling which would represent compensation in place of what would otherwise be a loss. If, in contrast, sterling's external value *appreciated* over the intervening three years – which it could well have done with this system's functioning – the then Bond-holders would reap in full the consequential advantages.

(c) However, it is highly improbable that the need would ever arise for any such deferring of payments. In the likely course of events, with seeming general world-commodity shortages (as reflected by abnormally high prices) obtaining in 1973–74, if this system were inaugurated by HM Government in 1975, a significant period might elapse before PSC was required to buy any commodity. But, in the light of past experiences, sooner or later it would commence to build up reserves of Commodities 'A', 'B', 'C' and 'D' without as yet holding any stocks of 'E' to (perhaps) 'Z'. In short, it would then have disbursed only a small fraction of the £90 million (9 per cent of a Key Control of £1,000 million – or similarly 9 per cent of a greater or less Key Control) that had been set as the limit on its cash-investments during the initial three years. Hence, in the circumstances likely to prevail during that period, it is highly improbable that the Chancellor of the Exchequer would have cause to direct that payments for purchases in excess of first BLOCKS (of, e.g., grains) should be deferred. Thus, in the happy event of widespread bountiful seasons leading to surpluses to then current demand – at not less than the relevant low *point(s)* – PSC could continue cash payments for series of BLOCKS of several products without its disbursements exceeding perhaps 20 to 30 per cent of £90 million – assuming £1,000 million to have been the Key Control.

B.11 EFFECT ON EXTERNAL BALANCE OF PAYMENTS OF THREE-YEAR BOND REDEMPTION. An obvious question arising is as to the effect on the external balance of payments in any year in which such Bonds (if issued) had to be redeemed. In the event, by the time any Bond had to be honoured, the nation would have acquired 100 per cent of its imported user-needs (in each of the three intervening years), in any commodity in respect of which a Bond had been issued, at an average price of 5 per cent below the average cost of such prices in the quinquennium prior to PSC's inception. Thus, if the average cost of annual imports of 'X' during that quinquennium had been £100 million, the same volumes in *each* of the three years following PSC's acquiring a first BLOCK of that commodity (and provided *some part* of that first BLOCK continued to be held by PSC) would probably have cost commercial buyers less by an average of 5 per cent in each of the intervening three years, representing a gross saving of some £15 million. In contrast the cost of Bond-redemption would be something less than £11,050,000, because that would be the redemption cost only in the event of a *full* BLOCK having been obtained against deferred payments. And, of course, if that had occurred, the cost per unit to commercial buyers would thereafter be still lower by an average of a further 5 per cent. The figure £11,050,000 is made up of Bonds to a face value of £8.5 million plus three years' interest at 10 per cent (not compounded) aggregating £11,050,000. If, in fact, PSC's holdings of any one commodity came to exceed a *third* full BLOCK there would be a further fall of 5 per cent in commercial cost because its Index and *points* would then have fallen *three times* by 5 per cent below initial levels.

B.12 PSC'S OUTLAY TO BE PREMIUM-EARNING. PSC's outlay would differ fundamentally from those forms of Governmental expenditure which are irrecoverable; because all moneys used in acquiring reserves would be investments secured on durable *essential* commodities. And, almost as surely as it had been required to buy at one period, so would it be required to sell at a later stage, and every sale would represent a gross premium of 22.2 per cent. If it were otherwise, it could only mean that commodity price stability (with all the consequential advantages – with money values virtually constant in terms of essential commodities) would have been achieved – with PSC continuing to hold stocks to ensure that such stability would be maintained.

And that is the objective of the whole exercise.

B.13 ATTITUDES OF OTHER INDUSTRIALIZED NATIONS.
(a) Another pertinent question arising is as to whether or not the Governments of other great commodity-importing countries would sit back and watch the United Kingdom establishing large reserves bought at 10 per cent below their preceding annual costs (over the quinquennium) when such commodities could not be bought from a British PSC excepting at the level of relevant HIGH *points*. In short, as soon as this system was seen to be functioning (or about to function) effectively in Britain, it would seem probable that other highly industrialized nations depending on external sources for basics would not be slow in setting up their own Price Stabilizing Authorities, a matter elaborated upon in Chapter 6 wherein it is shown that, far from being disadvantageous, this could be an unqualified boon to all – particularly the developing-nations.

(b) With this system being operated by two or more great commodity-importing nations (freight factors apart) the world floor price for 'X' would be the *highest* of the then low *points*; and the world ceiling price for 'X' would be the *lowest* of the then effective HIGH *points*. This is elaborated upon in Chapter 6.

B.14 PSC TO ACCEPT THE CUSTODY OF COMMERCIALLY-OWNED COMMODITIES.
(a) The following is a most important feature of this system's functioning, its purpose being (i) to foster the establishment of commercially-owned reserves; and (ii) to accord equal

bargaining powers (as in paragraph B.15) to producer-sellers and user-buyers. To these ends, PSC would stand ready to provide storage (*at net cost of space occupied*) for either producer-sellers, intermediaries, or user-industrialists, on precisely the same conditions (satisfactory pre-appraisal and delivery in pre-specified units-of-volume) as if such deposits were being sold to PSC instead of being lodged in its custody – a facility not to be confused with commercial warehousing.

(b) PSC's *Warrant* (receipt) for each such lodgement would be a firm security for Bank Loans up to near the level of the lodged commodity's low *point* at which it could be sold *in situ* for cash-sterling to PSC at any time, subject only to what appears in paragraph B.10, in respect of intakes exceeding first BLOCKS in the unlikely event of payments being deferred by the issue of Three-Year Bonds (not negotiable in the commercial sense); which Bonds are not to be confused with PSC's *Warrants*.

PROVISOS

Endorsed on each *Warrant* there would be two provisos as follows:

(i) If the price of any deposited commodity rise in any recognized British market above the level of that product's HIGH *point* (with PSC not holding reserves thereof in its *ownership*) the relevant *Warrant* becomes automatically void – when PSC forthwith pays the depositor at the level of the appropriate low *point* and holds that purchase available to the first-comer at its HIGH *point*.

(ii) Proviso (i) shall not apply in the case of a *bona fide* user-industrialist who has prudently established reserves (lodged with PSC) exclusively for his own use – and not to 'play the market' subject to PSC's being given what it would consider satisfactory assurances in this regard – see Chapter 3 (C.5).

B.15 EQUALIZING OF BARGAINING POWERS.

(a) The readiness of PSC to accept commercially-owned commodities as deposits against its negotiable *Warrants* affords to producer-sellers bargaining powers effectively to counteract the development of buyers' markets; and the holding by PSC of reserves (in its custody) likewise counteracts the development of sellers' markets.

(b) The significance of the foregoing requires emphasis for two special reasons; the first that it would ensure both producer-sellers and user-buyers having equal bargaining powers; and the second that – to the extent that (and for as long as) reserves were held in PSC's custody but commercial ownership – PSC would be relieved of the necessity to provide funds for the purchase of such reserves and would derive revenue from the payment to it of storage costs so incurred. Under such auspices, in the event of market offerings being apparently in excess of then current user-needs to the extent that a commodity's price fell to (or near to) the level of its relevant low *point*, selling pressure could quickly be relaxed by withdrawal from the market of such excess offerings as had been creating a buyers' market.

(c) While producers could sell their (excess) holdings wholly or in part to PSC, at the appropriate low *point*, it seems much more likely that they would lodge that 'excess' on deposit in PSC's custody when they could borrow from their banks against an absolutely firm security which could be exchanged *in situ* for cash up to the level of the then relevant low *point* as applied to the volume of whatever commodity was on deposit. If this situation be thought through it will show that, with the entirely novel feature of producer-sellers and user-buyers having equalized bargaining powers, the net result would probably be that prices would tend to remain very close to the level of the relevant Index; i.e., midway between the low and (effective) HIGH *points*.

(d) It is conceivable that, by such tactics, producer-sellers if working in close combination might be able to ensure a constant sellers' market but only up to the level of the relevant HIGH *point* which, if exceeded in the market, would lead to the immediate take-over by PSC of relevant deposits in its custody, with payment at the appropriate low *point*, when it would stand ready to sell to first-comers at the level of the then HIGH *point*.

(e) The strong probability is that the result of all this would be that (excepting in cases of *real* shortage) market prices (brokerage and handling charges aside) would seldom be higher or lower by more than perhaps 5 per cent than the price level represented by PSC's Index of the commodity concerned.

(f) In this regard it is safe to assume that user-buyers would not regard the selling by producers to PSC at the low *point* with any enthusiasm; because if at a later date user-buyers had to purchase from PSC they would have to pay at the level of the then HIGH *point*. Hence, it would seem likely that (when there was an excess of market offerings) buyers would make the best possible bargain with sellers and themselves deposit their resulting holdings in PSC custody using their *Warrants* as security for bank loans if they so wished. Such trading could be in 'deposits *in situ*' – with withdrawals only when required for usage.

(g) It would be as salutary as it was novel for basic producer-sellers to have the same bargaining counters as user-buyers. A constant margin of 22.2 per cent of the relevant low *point* between that and the then HIGH *point* should provide ample scope for the legitimate functioning of intermediaries.

B.16 OVERALL GUIDE FOR BASIC PRODUCERS. The extent of a surplus (if it occurs) of Commodity 'X' provides a self-evident guide to producers thereof; and if – over the longish term – reserves of 'X' increase, a proportion of the capital and enterprise devoted to producing 'X' will be diverted to producing other commodities of which no reserves (or only occasional small reserves) have been established under PSC auspices.

Thereby something approaching well-balanced production of basics would come about gradually but surely.

B.17 ENTREPÔT TRADING FACILITATED. The holding of reserves in custody for commercial owners would greatly facilitate expansions of entrepôt trading by British mercantile interests whose experience in this field is perhaps unique – and for which Britain is ideally situated geographically.

B.18 ALL HOLDINGS TO BE INCLUDED IN ASSESSING BLOCKS. In regularly publicizing its commodity holdings (the precise extent of which could be ascertained on enquiry at any time) PSC would state the volumes held in its ownership and (separately) in its custody but in commercial ownership. However, both its own reserves and those held merely on deposit would be taken into account when assessing **BLOCK**-accumulations – if any.

B.19 COUNTER-INFLATIONARY FACTORS AT BASE OF ECONOMY. (a) If PSC were not called upon to function no investment-expenditure would be involved. If it *was* called upon to act there would automatically be achieved a degree of price stability, that had not theretofore obtained, for each commodity it took into its reserves; that is, for as long as it so held reserves. Moreover, the greater the volume of such reserves – beyond a first BLOCK of any commodity – the cheaper would be the average cost per unit of that product compared with the average of its cost during the preceding period of years on which the relevant *initial* Valorizing Index had been based.

(b) If industrialists were positively assured of continuity of supply of their raw materials within precisely predictable (relatively narrow) limits of market price movements – as they would be so long as PSC held relevant reserves – they would be in a position correspondingly to stabilize the selling prices of their finished products to *the extent to which their costs depended on what they had had to pay for their raw materials.* In this regard, as matters stand, when there is a steep rise in costs of a basic product the user-industrialists concerned normally seek to 'absorb' this without its being carried forward to the price of the finished article – which is prudently set at a level that enables that to be done. But – to the extent that this entails a lowering of profits – there is a limit to such indulgence beyond which increased raw-material costs must be passed on to the consumer. However – in existing circumstances – it certainly does not follow that a sudden fall (however considerable) in raw-product costs will result in the price of the finished article being lowered. Manufacturers are compelled to play for safety, and it is not usual for (probably temporary) declines in raw-material costs to be reflected in lower prices of finished goods. However, if they did not have to gear their costings to cope with unpredictably high raw material prices, and could rely on continuity of supply within a known narrow 'price band', they could adjust the initial phase of their costings accordingly – to the advantage of the ultimate consumer-buyer.

(c) While in certain sectors of manufacturing, such costs (especially of metals and textiles) loom large, basic-material costs decrease in importance in inverse ratio to the extent of fabrication involved in producing finished products. Thus, in varying degrees, the wage-and-salary cost is usually the most important factor in respect of determining profitable selling prices. In this context, all that can be said in that regard is that such justification as obtains for constantly increasing remuneration demands – unless matched by increased productivity – would have less strength in proportion to any stabilization of (or reduction in) costs of foodstuffs and in selling prices of essential manufactures to the extent that raw-material costs had been stabilized – if not reduced.

B.20 HOW BASIC PRODUCERS WOULD FARE.

(a) It would be grossly improper to suggest that an ultimate purpose of the proposed system would be to reduce the incomes of producers of commodities within PSC's scope. From the outset such producers would have the unprecedented boon of there being floors in markets close to the level of each commodity's low *point – a type of premium-free insurance.* Thus the producer of 'X' would receive his full returns from all his commercial sales; and, if the output of producers as-a-whole of 'X' exceeded buyers' then requirements (at prices not less than 'X''s low *point*), instead of this causing unbridled market depression, such then excess to current usage could be sold to PSC with the certainty that PSC could not re-sell excepting at a price higher by 22.2 per cent (if the proposed gearing had been adopted) than that which it had paid. Hence producers of 'X' would obtain income not only from their commercial sales but also from their disposals (if any) to PSC.

(b) Of course, if PSC's purchases came to aggregate a first BLOCK of 'X' (one-tenth of the UK's preceding annual imports) there would be a 5 per cent fall in that commodity's Index and *points* – whereby its average cost to the user-industrialist would be less by that percentage than the average corresponding cost over the preceding period of years on which 'X''s *initial* Index had been based.

(c) It must be emphasized that basic producers as-a-whole of any 'eligible' commodity would be the sole arbiters as to the extent to which their interests would be best served, in which regard they would have the following options:

(i) to restrict their productive enterprise so as to diminish outputs and maintain high price levels – *which they are free to do in any event*;

(ii) to produce – wittingly or unwittingly – above the then anticipated needs of user-industries at prices not less than the relevant low *points* and to dispose of surpluses (to current market absorption) to PSC; or

(iii) themselves to hold such 'surpluses' unremuneratively – as dead weight, or to sell them for what they would fetch.

In the event it would seem likely that they would have recourse to (ii) and that this system would function as intended.

B.21 WHY WHAT IS ADVOCATED IS TERMED A SYSTEM.
(a) To describe the adoption of these proposals as initiating a *plan* could be somewhat misleading; because, it is reiterated, PSC is *per se* inert. In fact it is analogous to a clock which, though in good mechanical order, will not function unless it is actuated by 'winding'. It is not a clock which *plans* one's day; it is the position of its 'hands' which is our guide in allocating our time – although if the 'hands' be of a Bundy clock one has but small say in the matter!

(b) In a similar sense PSC cannot operate unless *it* has been actuated in the first instance by willing sellers – whose prime consideration is their own best interest. Its *raison d'être* is to stand ready (in the background) to put into effect a *system* the functioning of which makes evident the supply and demand situation in respect of Commodity 'X' as clearly as do the hands of a clock denote the time. It would be in such circumstances that both basic producers *and* user-industrialists would themselves be able to make their own *plans* – with a measure of confidence for which, theretofore, there had been no firm grounds.

(c) It may have been noted that PSC's reserves are not referred to at any stage as 'buffer stocks'. This is to avoid confusion with such schemes as that of the International Tin Council whose Buffer Stock Manager *enters* the market as either buyer or seller of tin at his discretion – see Chapter 7 – which is something PSC would never do.

B.22 THE ELEMENT OF CONTAGION. There is a strong element of contagion in respect of irrational commodity-price fluctuation, especially when prices rise precipitately in periods of extreme tensions – either national or domestic; usually only to fall with even greater precipitation when such tensions relax. The greater the volumes and diversity of reserves held under PSC's auspices, the less would be the likelihood of such economy-disrupting incidence. There is likewise a considerable element of contagion in respect of price stability; that is to say, if there be stability in markets for *durable* basics, this will extend to a significant extent to many products not physically eligible to be brought within this system's scope. In this regard one example may suffice.

> The cost of production of many animal-products, e.g., meats, dairy products, poultry and eggs (all naturally perishable and ineligible for inclusion within PSC's scope unless susceptible to some *economical* form of preservation), are largely dependent on the costs of animal feeding-stuffs of types that would qualify for inclusion within PSC's scope.

> Many other examples might be cited, some obvious and others not so obvious – but nonetheless advantageous.

B.23 POSSIBLE EXTENSION OF RANGE OF 'ELIGIBLES'. That naturally perishable products preserved by dehydration, canning, refrigeration, or other means, might ultimately be brought within PSC's scope is debatable. It would be prudent to limit the range of eligibles to durable (or near durable) commodities at the outset. However, in the light of experience, preserved perishables might be included as indeed might first-processed durable commodities such as steel in those basic forms which are raw materials for fabricating industries.

B.24 IMPORTANT QUALIFICATION AS TO FOREGOING TEXT. It is to be particularly emphasized that the foregoing text is designed to be basically *illustrative* in respect of such tentative suggestions as the following:

(a) that the sum £1,000 million (or £2,000 million) be taken as the Key Control figure;

(b) as to the setting of the *initial* Index and levels of *points* – especially *with due regard to inflation-weighting*;

(c) as to the volume in reserve (of any product) which might aggregate a BLOCK – with resulting adjustment in its Index-and-*points* levels; and,

(d) as to the percentages by which such adjustments might be effected.

The prime purpose of the author is to make clear the underlying *principles* which would govern this system's effective functioning.

What is of overriding importance is that:

(i) all such details should have been determined and publicized at date of the Statutory inauguration of (what is here termed) a Price Stabilizing Corporation; and,

(ii) that such details should be simple and devoid of ambiguity.

Nevertheless, it may be that those directly concerned would consider the illustrative figures in this text (inflation-weighted if necessary) as not being wide-of-the-mark.

B.25 WHY DOMESTICALLY-PRODUCED BASICS ARE EXCLUDED.
It will not have escaped notice that this proposal is designed to have applicability only to (physically suitable) *imported* basic commodities – and that domestically-produced commodities are excluded. The reason is that, within the UK and many other advanced countries, domestic primary producers are normally protected against unremunerative prices.* In some instances (in certain countries) such policies have been described – and with ample justification – as feather-bedding. Of course, any nation adopting this system would be free to make it applicable to its own domestic products; but it would tend to befog the whole issue (so far as a British PSC was

*Or they were until the inflated costs of feeding-stuffs for livestock so rocketed in 1973/74 that British farmers were producing at a loss. It is not known at time of writing what HMG will do in this matter but it would seem that the live-stock subsidy should be geared to the cost of feeding stuffs.

concerned) for a recommendation to that end to be included in this thesis.

B.26 RECOURSE TO PSC NOT LIKELY TO BE FREQUENT.   In the event it would seem that only in exceptional circumstances would PSC be required actually to *buy* a commodity; but that would certainly not mean that it had failed in its purpose. In contrast, it would seem highly likely that – in the early years following its inception – it would fairly frequently be approached to accept the custody of commercially owned deposits – for the reasons set out in paragraph B.15. Nevertheless it will be manifest that PSC's constant readiness to function would have an unprecedentedly-steadying effect on world markets; and that the wider the range of commodities brought within its scope, the greater would be its stabilizing influence.

B.27 RESERVOIR ANALOGY. Far more water is precipitated on London and the Home Counties in a normal year than is required by their over 20 million inhabitants. But what would be our predicament if, having installed an efficient system of pipe distribution, we neglected to establish and maintain reservoirs holding sufficient to ensure continuity of water supply?

The logic, practicability and economic validity of the proposed system rests upon that analogy, subject to what appears in Chapter 5 (E.28 onwards) in respect of wasting assets.

3. Administration – Simple and Economical

C.1 A COMPACT ORGANIZATION.

(a) *The Board:* Administrative control would be vested in a Statutorily appointed Board comprising a Chairman and maybe two or three part-time members (who might or might not be commodity experts) responsible to the Chancellor of the Exchequer. Ordinarily passive, it would stand ready to function, virtually automatically, as and when the need arose. Its specific duties are suggested in paragraph C.5.

(b) *Permanent Staff:* This would comprise a Manager who would require only a very small regular staff even when PSC came to active functioning. At the outset there would be collected and correlated all available estimates of future world productive capacity in respect of every commodity with which PSC would be concerned – of each product which had been conditionally valorized as described in Chapter 2. Such data could be obtained from the UN Food and Agriculture Organization and from such bodies as the International Organizations dealing with grain, sugar, coffee, cocoa and other basic foods; and with kindred bodies concerned with metals, textile raw materials, rubber and other basics. Special regard would be paid to forecasts as to seasonal conditions (as applicable) in the principal producing countries. The Board would be advised accordingly so as to be in a position to decide if and when it would be necessary to arrange for the provision of commodity reception depots as in C.2.

(c) *Specialists:* The permanent staff would not include any of the various specialists whose services would be required from time to time. Instead, nominal retaining fees would be paid to panels of experts whose services when called upon would be paid for on a fee-for-service basis. They would include such professionals as land-valuers, building surveyors and architects, as well as expert appraisers of all the commodities within PSC's scope. It would be desirable that all these panels should be nominated by the professional or trade associations concerned. The services would similarly be retained of scientists competent to deal with problems that might arise regarding possible deterioration of some types of commodities (e.g., grains) when held in reserve.

Thus would PSC's overhead expenditure be constantly kept at a minimum.

(d) *Office Accommodation:* Unless prestige factors otherwise required (and there is no reason why they should) the Board and its staff could be accommodated in a very small suite of offices – even if and when it was involved in considerable transactions.

C.2 STORAGE FACILITIES. PSC would not have recourse to the construction of storage depots if it were able to acquire existing accommodation that could be adapted to its special requirements. If it had to construct its own reception depots these would be sited – as far as practicable – to suit the pre-ascertained convenience of the trades concerned. They would be constructed so as to ensure absolute security without requiring custodians; that is, with ordinary police vigilance sufficing. They would be without windows though ventilated and (if essential) air-conditioned. In some cases – especially for metals – they would be underground. All would be compartmented into sections each designed to contain one of the units-of-volume which PSC would purchase or sell (or accept on deposit (as in C.3).

Although types of stores would naturally vary to accommodate different sorts of commodities, each would conform to specified standards. In some instances facilities would be installed for movements of commodities from delivering vehicles to allotted spaces; in other cases PSC might have a standing agreement with concerns that operate that sort of (mobile) equipment. But in no circumstances would PSC meet any costs so involved, all of which would have to be borne by the seller, depositor or buyer concerned.

When commercially-owned commodities were accepted on

deposit the rental charge would be based on the (financial servicing) cost of the space occupied which would have to be at least that required for one unit-of-volume of whatever was the product so lodged. Depositor would be responsible for effecting insurance. However, because there would be no attendant staff, the overall cost would be incomparably less than that of commercial warehousing.

In the selection of sites for its depots and in respect of their external appearance, PSC would have constant regard for environmental considerations.

From time to time in past decades I have had firm estimates from eminent constructional authorities, such as Oscar Faber and Partners, Taylor Woodrow and John Laing and Company as to the costs of erecting stores. In the early sixties these ranged from £5 per ton-capacity for metals to £20 for textile raw materials. But in the circumstances obtaining at time of writing it is doubtful that any firm would venture to provide an estimate as to what construction costs would be when the time came for stores to be built. However, the apparent current shortage of commercially-owned reserves is such that, if PSC were established in 1975, there would probably be ample existing empty storage space available for it to acquire and adapt to its special requirements.

C.3 TRANSACTIONAL PROCEDURES.

(a) *Prescribed Units-of-Volume:* It is reiterated that PSC would accept on deposit or buy and (later) sell only in prescribed units-of-volume (not to be confused with BLOCKS which would contain several hundred such units-of-volume), perhaps 20-ton lots of, e.g., copper (of which as the annual average import by the UK is around 500,000 tons, a BLOCK would aggregate 50,000 tons); and of other specified volumes of other commodities.

Reference in Chapter 7 to the functioning of the International Tin Council will show that in administering its buffer-stock scheme it stipulates that 'the minimum tonnage of all trans-actions shall be five tons, and larger tonnages shall be in multiples of five tons'. However, it is unlikely that the units-of-volume which PSC would buy or sell would be so small. It would seem more likely that such units would be of 20-tons or perhaps of higher volumes.

N.B. The reason an intending depositor of a commodity in PSC's custody would have to conform precisely to the procedure applicable to sellers to PSC is that it would always stand ready to buy any such lodgement *in situ* if the necessity arose, as it might do if the depositor used his *Warrant* as security for a bank loan which he failed to repay, in which event his bank could at once surrender that *Warrant* to PSC for cash at the deposit's low *point* value.

(b) *Adequate Notice Required:* A specified period of notice (maybe seven days – or longer) would be required of an intending vendor's wish to sell to (or of a depositor's wish to lodge with) PSC – with advice as to the then location of the offering.

(c) *Appraisal at Vendor's (or Depositor's) Cost:* Vendor (or depositor) would be required to pay (to PSC) the cost of appraisal (irrespective of the outcome), to be carried out in the presence of PSC's representative. *If an offering did not survive appraisal it would be refused.*

(d) *Delivery to be Vendor's (or Depositor's) Responsibility:* If appraisal was satisfactory, the onus and cost of delivering each acceptable unit-of-volume to its specified (numbered) compartment – under supervision of the appraiser and of PSC's representative – would rest wholly with the vendor (or depositor).

(e) *Buyers to Collect:* The onus and cost of collecting any purchase (or of removing any deposited commodity) would rest wholly upon the buyer (or on the depositor).

C.4 COUNTERING DETERIORATION – IF APPLICABLE. Effective methods would be in readiness (under specialist direction as required) to counteract deterioration of such few eligible commodities (e.g., grains) as were susceptible thereto.

If there were any doubt as to the efficacy of corrective measures, the affected units in reserve would at once be sold (by agents acting for PSC) for what they would fetch. But, concurrently, PSC – by its agents – would purchase a precisely similar volume of that commodity in the market. Such would be the only occasions when PSC might (obliquely) enter the market which, however, would not be disturbed because the volume sold would be precisely off-set by the volume purchased. This practice, known as 'stock-rotation', has long been followed by the Ministry responsible for the maintenance of strategic reserves. No doubt some loss would be sustained in such circumstances; but close supervision and care of stocks would ensure that any losses due to deterioration would not be serious.

C.5 DUTIES OF THE BOARD. It would be for the Board to ensure that the greatest practicable economy should be exercised in all aspects of PSC's administration, and in respect of the provision of storage. It would be required to take decisions as to the acceptance or otherwise of assurances by user-industrialists who deposited their own reserves in PSC's custody as required by proviso (ii) in paragraph B.14 of Chapter 2; and to tender advice and make recommendations to the Chancellor of the Exchequer in such matters as the possible inclusion within PSC's scope of commodities not initially so included.

C.6 NO SCOPE FOR THE BUREAUCRAT.
(a) If the foregoing text has been explicitly clear, it will have been appreciated that there would be no scope whatever for bureaucracy on the part of PSC's staff, whose duties would virtually be as uncomplicated as those of Post Office counter-staff, albeit in reverse.

A Post Office clerk supplies a money order for £1, charging that sum plus $2\frac{1}{2}$ per cent (termed poundage); while he stands ready to 'buy' a money order for £1 at its precise face value, it is not for him to 'bargain' – nor would it be for any PSC official. Subject to satisfactory pre-appraisal (for which PSC's permanent officials would not be responsible) and to the other conditions specified above, its staff will pay for Commodity 'X' at its then Index value minus 10 per cent; and thereafter (for so long as stocks of 'X' are held in PSC's ownership) will stand ready to sell it on demand at its then Index value plus 10 per cent.

It is as simple as that – with no scope provided for Professor Parkinson's fun.

(b) The fact that – though of the greatest importance in practical terms – this is the shortest chapter in this book will not escape notice; and it may be that, in the estimation of certain critics, it represents an over-simplification. But, perhaps, when anyone of that mind comes to read Chapter 7 treating of the Intricacies of International Commodity Agreements, he will change his mind. Let it not be thought that the author is without administrative experience. The fact is that in addition to having been a producer and seller of a wide range of basics, I have also had considerable experience in business enterprises as well as in the public sector in that I have held responsible posts in the Civil Services of both Australia and the United Kingdom. In both these latter spheres the significance of my experience was – for a great part – that I learnt what was to be avoided in the way of wasteful expenditure.

4. Illustrating the System in Operation

FORENOTE. That parts of what now follows are repetitive is because earlier sections require elaboration.

D.1 CONFIDENCE NEEDS TO BE INSPIRED.

(a) This chapter shows, in principle, precisely how the functioning of a British Price Stabilizing Corporation would provide assurances to primary producers of a wide range of commodities that they could embark upon programmes greatly to increase their outputs with a measure of confidence that had never theretofore obtained; that is (it is reiterated) with a premium-free insurance that, under this system's auspices, there would be no risk of future precipitate price decline below prenotified minimum levels. With PSC in the background there would always be known floors in British (and world) markets, with reductions (if any) in such floor-levels accurately predictable and by percentages that were literally negligible as compared with what had so often occurred in the then past. Furthermore, their own bargaining power would be immeasurably strengthened – as in B.15.

(b) To reduce the whole procedure to the simplest terms, suppose – as already indicated in Chapter 2 (B.5): (i) that the preceding annual average imports of 'X' had been 500,000 tons whereby a BLOCK of 'X' would be 50,000 tons; and (ii) *initial* Index (annual average preceding costs cif per ton, inflation- and freight-cost-weighted if so prescribed) were £100 per ton, with its low *point* at £90 and its conditional HIGH *point* at £110 per ton. Of course, unless and until PSC acquired reserves, prices would be free to rise to any levels buyers were prepared to pay. But, if and as soon as PSC came to hold reserves of 'X' – making the HIGH *point* effective –

there would then be a market ceiling at £110 for as long as any part of such reserves were so held. Producers' receipts would be what they had obtained from ordinary commercial sales *plus* what they received for disposals to PSC – or in the form of bank loans against their *Warrants* if they lodged deposits with PSC. And, until and unless a first BLOCK of 'X' came to be held, as an aggregate of PSC's purchases (and/or lodgement in its custody) market prices would be free to rise to the level of the HIGH *point* at £110.

(c) Now let it be assumed that supplies coming forward within (say) the first year following PSC's inception aggregated 580,000 tons of which ordinary commercial sales absorbed 550,000 tons (assuming real demand to have increased by 10 per cent above previous annual average) at prices never less than £90 per ton. Obviously, if the extra 30,000 tons were on offer for what these would fetch – i.e., if PSC were not in the background – there would be serious price recession but, in the event, producers would doubtless have recourse to PSC – either lodging their excess (market depressing) supplies on deposit with PSC (as in B.14) or selling these wholly – or in part – to PSC. Thereby, they would, of course, be establishing a market ceiling at £110; but their bargaining powers (as in B.15) would be such that the average of their receipts from commercial sales would probably be around the level of the Index at £100 per ton. If so they would derive £550 million – leaving 30,000 tons which they could dispose of to PSC at £90 per ton (i.e., for £2,700,000), thereby making their total receipts £57,700,000. Producers could continue selling to (or depositing with) PSC – the low *point* standing at £90 – until such disposals had aggregated 50,000 tons making a first full BLOCK of 'X'. Thereupon its Index and *points* would fall automatically by 5 per cent when the market ceiling would become £104.5 and the market floor £85.5. Thus, even if two full BLOCKS accumulated in PSC reserve – with the Index falling to £90, the low *point* to £81 and the HIGH *point* to £99, commercial prices (probably averaging around the central figure of £90) might still rise to the HIGH *point* at only £1 per ton less than the *initial* Index level at £100 per ton.

(d) In short, a surplus to user-industry requirements equivalent to 20 per cent by volume would have been absorbed by PSC with a fall in the average of *commercial* prices of only 10 per cent. It may be salutary to contemplate what sort of a slump would occur if there were a 20 per cent physical surplus to real effective consumer demand and there were no PSC to stop the rot.

(e) Let it be kept in mind that no agreement is called for in respect of the foregoing and that there are no controls or regulations imposed by PSC. Natural hazards apart, producers of basics become controllers of their own destinies under this system's wholly impartial aegis.

D.2 FUTURE PROSPECTS. An attempt is made in Chapter 5 to gauge the future general world supply potential in respect of the types of products mentioned therein of which some might well be in excess-supply at some stage in 1975, because of the unwonted stimulus to producers accorded by the un-precedentedly high prices as here discussed. By excess-supply, one means that the actual volume of a commodity produced in (say) a single year on a world basis, exceeds actual effective (commercial) demand; and by effective demand is here meant market absorption at prices not lower than those which would be assured to the producer under PSC auspices.

D.3 THE OVERALL PICTURE AS IN LATE 1974. Thus far – as in Chapter 2 (B.2) – a Key Control of £1,000 million has been taken as a convenient figure from which to present the simple calculations to illustrate the gearing of the proposed system: i.e., how Index-and-*points* adjustment would come into effect. However, as was stated earlier, such adjustments would be *pro rata* in respect of any greater (or less) Key Control. Further to that qualification, there are tabulated on page 70 (overleaf) the (estimated) costs cif of fifteen important essential basic imported commodities over the quinquennium 1970 to 1974 inclusive. The word 'estimated' is used because, at time of writing, the relevant external trade figures thus far available for 1974 cover only the period up to the end of June. Hence, in order to arrive at a realistic total as a basis for establishing an *initial* Index (for each of these commodities) to have applicability in early 1975, the import figures for the

Trial illustration to arrive at a Key Control figure of £1,200 million based on annual averages of CIF costs of 15 major commodity imports during the quinquennium 1970 to 1974 inclusive. *But see* N.B. *page 27, and* B.4.

N.B. As figures currently available (late September) for 1974 are for the first half year only, for 1974 as a whole figures are estimated at double those of the first half year subject to subsequent minor adjustment, but such revisions will not significantly affect the overall picture.

ANNUAL AVERAGE IMPORTS

	Volume	Gross cost	Average per ton CIF	Initial index (rounded)	Low point	High* point	Size of BLOCK	Investment to acquire first full BLOCKS	Selling value of same
	'000 tons	£m	£				'000 tons	£m	£m
WHEAT	4,016	163	49	£50	£45	£55	400	18	22
MAIZE	3,137	122	38	£40	£36	£44	300	10.8	13.2
SUGAR	1,865	130.8	69	£70	£63	£77	200	12.6	15.4
COFFEE	109	49	443	£450	£405	£495	11	4.45	5.44
COCOA	98.7	38	371	£370	£343	£407	10	3.43	4.07
WOOL	298	126	564	£560	£504	£616	30	15.12	18.48
COTTON	234.4	62	275	£270	£243	£297	24	5.83	7.13
JUTE	77	11	145	£140	£126	£154	7.7	0.97	1.19
RUBBER	186	42.2	228	£230	£207	£253	19	3.93	4.81
OIL SEEDS AND NUTS**	134.7	17.9	132.6	£130	£117	£143	13	1.53	1.86
SOYA BEANS	555.5	42.6	68.9	£70	£63	£77	55	3.46	4.23
COPPER	434	280	645	£640	£576	£704	44	25.34	30.98
LEAD	220	43.2	201	£200	£180	£220	22	3.96	4.84
TIN	6.6	13.1	1,996	£2,000	£1,800	£2,200	0.66	1.19	1.45
ZINC	195	38.9	198	£200	£180	£220	20	3.6	4.4
								(a)	(a)

Total of 5-year average annual costs   £1,179.7

Therefore call Key Control: £1,200 million;   Possible Investment in first full BLOCK series £108m;   Selling Value £132m – at which Gross Premium £24m.

SOURCE: 'Overseas Trade Statistics of the United Kingdom'. The returns for 1970, 1971 and 1972 are in tons and for 1973 and 1974 in tonnes but for the purpose of this example these have been taken as equal.
(a) Discrepancies in the totals of the 8th and 9th columns (if these had been given) would be due to the rounding-off (for convenient reckoning of the *initial* Index figures in the 4th column).
* High *point* is effective only when reserves come to be held.
** Oil seeds and nuts are groundnuts, copra and palm kernels only. Each would have its own Index and points—as would recognized

first half of 1974 are doubled. But, because the cif costs of many of the commodities named are likely to be substantially lower in the second (than in the first) half of 1974, any error would be reflected by a lower Key Control than £1,200 million (£1,180 rounded upwards). Be that as it may that sum could result (as shown) in a remotely possible cash-investment by PSC of an aggregate of around £108 million; that is supposing it established reserves equivalent to a first FULL-BLOCK-SERIES.

Given that the reader examines the details as tabulated he may conclude that it would be unlikely that PSC would acquire *any* reserves of this or that commodity with its initial low *point* at the level shown. In this respect two important factors have to be kept in mind. The first is the elasticity of this system which means in effect that if Parliament so decided (when framing the enabling Statute) each *initial* Index could be set at higher than the illustrative levels. Thus it could be based (perhaps) on the immediately preceding *three year* averages (as in B.7(a)); or, alternatively, there could be a general weighting in compensation for overall inflation (as in B.4(a)). But it is again stressed that, whatever was the established *initial* Index, it should not be altered (excepting in prespecified stages in reverse ratio to accumulations, if any) without amending legislation (as in B.3(b)).

The second factor is that due regard should be paid to what appears in Chapter 5 which deals at some length with the potential for increasing outputs of every commodity brought within PSC's scope.

D.4 POSSIBLE EXTENSION OF RANGE OF COMMODITIES VALORIZED.

(a) It will be seen that very many essential imported commodities such as iron ore and pig iron, timber and wood pulp and various raw materials for the chemical industry – *inter alia* – do not figure in the tabulated list. If all these were so included the Key Control might need to be raised to £2,000 million, in which event the investment involved for PSC to acquire a first FULL-BLOCK-SERIES would become 9 per cent of that figure, i.e., £180 million. However, the inclusion of some such other commodities would present difficulties as to the setting of the relevant *initial* Index; because, as examples, iron ore has a wide range of ferrous content, and timber is imported in a great many shapes and sizes. Nevertheless in the light of experience the list of commodities brought within PSC's scope might later be greatly expanded. Suffice it to say here that, if and when there had come about realistic stabilization of costs of the commodities listed (or of some of them) it might well be decided to bring a number of others within this system's range.

(b) It will have been noted that petroleum is not mentioned for the perhaps obvious reason that its cost is extremely unlikely to fall to what would become its low *point*. However, who is to say what may be in prospect in the light of the frequencies of discoveries of 'new' deposits – a theme elaborated upon in Chapter 5 (E.29).

(c) Reverting to the tabulated items on page 70 it might well prove that PSC would not be required to *purchase* any part of a first BLOCK of any single commodity during the first year (or more) of its standing ready to operate. But that would most certainly not mean that it had failed to achieve its first objective; because – be it reiterated – that first objective is to inspire confidence among basic producers (the world over) of every commodity within its range. Producers would be aware that, however much greater their outputs were than market absorption at not less than the relevant low *point*, all otherwise-market-depressing 'surpluses' could be exchanged for sterling; or (if consigned to other industrialized nations) other currencies.

(d) Thereby producers would be accorded reciprocal buying power – *additional to what they had acquired by commercial selling* – and they would doubtless be quick to utilize this· Moreover they would surely have a predisposition to purchase manufactures – and services – in the country whose currency had thus been made accessible to them. Furthermore, the greater the demand for manufactures so engendered, the greater the demand for raw materials – of which reserves would then be held under PSC auspices. In these circumstances industrialists would be assured of continuity of supply within known 'price bands'; and that would go far towards enabling them the more confidently to stabilize their selling prices – at least to the extent that these had been costed on the price they had had to pay for their raw materials.

D.5 SPECULATION UNBRIDLED. Some comment on what actually happened in respect of a few commodities would here seem opportune.

> **Copper:** Although there was an increase in imports of this metal from 442,000 tons in 1972 (by 5.4%) to 466,000 in 1973, its price on the London Metal Exchange rose from £454 per ton in January of the latter year to £1,135 in December – an increase of 150 per cent. Within the first eleven months of 1974 it was down to £877 in January, up to £1,400 in April, and down to £564 in October.

> **Zinc:** Imports during 1972 at 227,000 tons fell to 226,000 (or by less than 0.5%) in 1973; yet its LME price rose from £163 a ton in January (by 450%) to £938 in December. Within the first eleven months of 1974 it ranged from £875 in May to £319 in October.

> **Lead:** Imports in 1972 had been 204,000 tons, but these increased in 1973 to 216,000 tons. Nevertheless, its LME price rose from £133 during January to £330 in December. Within the first eleven months of 1974 the price range was from £324 in February to £217 in July.

> **Tin:** The imports of tin-metal in 1972 at 6,700 tons were within a hundred tons of volume imported in 1973. In the event its price rose from £1,620 during January to £3,190 in December. Up to October 1974 the range on the LME was from £4,200 in September to £2,930 in October.

D.6 A CONFESSION OF BEWILDERMENT. One is not so venturesome as to attempt to estimate the effect of pure speculation in these connexions. However, the reader may find that interest attaches to the following London Metal Exchange statistics.

LME TURNOVER – 1973 (tonnes)

Copper		Lead	Zinc	Tin
Wirebars	*Cathodes*			
4,289,550	386,575	1,341,325	1,324,575	169,250

With these figures before me I drew certain conclusions which I sent to a friend who is a recognized high authority in these respects, asking for his criticism. I got it! I need not quote what I had written because that can be inferred from his reply which reads:

In the paper you sent me with your letter you are so far off-beam that I have to try to correct some basic misapprehensions as to what terminal markets are all about. 'Fictional trading' is a completely incorrect term. A terminal market exists in order to carry out three basic functions: (i) *Pricing* – without the high turnover in deals where there need not actually be any movement of the goods, there could be no yardstick for any of the direct producer to consumer business done across the world on the basis of free-market prices as opposed to cartel prices. There would also be no facility for (ii) *Hedging*. Here a producer, fabricator, merchant or broker (or plumber's merchant for that matter) may protect himself against the effect of adverse price movements which might occur between inception and execution of a forward commitment. He does this by entering into an equal-and-opposite deal forward on the market; when the physical deal is timed for execution, the market 'paper' deal is cancelled-out by buying or selling against it, and losses on the one will be offset by profits on the other. Thus there have been two market deals to hedge one physical one: without hedging thus, the person concerned would have been uncovered and indeed would have been speculating! (iii) Finally, the market acts as a physical *market of last resort*. All LME contracts envisage physical delivery if they run to maturity, and there is no *force majeure* clause in them. In terms of turnover, this last function is the least one, though the run downs of LME copper stocks over 1973 from 180,000 to 30,000 tons shows that a lot of metal actually moved.

You are also at fault in assuming that UK imports alone make up the LME turnover. We are an international market and do an enormous third-country trade. This also has its effect on our contribution to the country's invisible earnings. Don't forget, for example, both China and Japan buying and hedging on the LME and paying in sterling in London!

No doubt my friend's reproof will be seen, by those sophisticated in such matters, to have been well-deserved. But I confess to continuing bafflement which has since been in no sense alleviated by my reading an article 'Five-Minute Bedlam in a Fair Market' in *The Times* (9/10/74) by its Commodities Editor (Mr John Woodland) from which the following are excerpts:

Precisely at noon on each business day some 30 dealers – with their assistants – gather in a small corner of London. They sit in a circle while copper prices are shouted across the floor of the 'ring'. At 12.05 the first copper call ends. In these five minutes thousands of tons can change hands. The money value runs into millions of pounds.

Frequently the noise is deafening . . . dealers seemingly tense with excitement. For the uninitiated it is bedlam and incomprehensible. *Yet, from this extraordinary event the world's copper price evolves.* This is flashed across the globe via telex, telephone and news agencies; and producers, consumers, merchants and dealers know almost instantly whether the price is right for them to buy . . . sell . . . or wait.

Further five minute calls are made at [specified intervals] up to 4.20 p.m.

In price terms copper has been through the most bizarre period. At the beginning of 1973 with the price in the middle £400's, nobody would have dreamt of a £750 price, let alone a £1,000 price a tonne. *Yet, on 1 April 1974 the cash wire price was traded at an all time high of £1,410.* . . . Currency crises inevitably appeared which caused speculators to enter metal markets – and copper in particular – to find a safer haven for their funds rather than to hold paper money which may have been devalued overnight. . . . With production troubles galore, stocks were rapidly reduced. On 2 December 1972 the London Metal Exchange warehouses held a record 192,100 tons. By June, 1973, they had fallen to 42,325 tons and in March, 1974, they were almost at a crisis level of 10,475 tons.

One thing is certain: the utility value of this metal remained constant throughout. Of course what occurred on the LME was a reflection of what was happening in American (and other) metal markets or *vice versa*.

D.7 CONTRAST – UNDER THE AEGIS OF THE *Producers' Price.* In this context during the period 1960 and 1963 there was in operation in respect of virgin copper what was termed a

Producers' Price – in fact a contract between overseas producers exporting to the United Kingdom and copper-using industrialists in this country. For some four years this cut out recourse to the London Metal Exchange in respect of other than small quantities of this metal, perhaps re-cycled scrap or maybe from sellers who were not parties to the *Producers' Price* arrangement. In the event, during 1960 (in which year the cif cost of 556,000 tons of copper imported was £248 per ton) the minimum price on the LME was £218 and the maximum £280 – an actual margin of £62 per ton or 28 per cent. During the succeeding three years the annual average imports were 520,000 tons at an average cif cost of £232; and throughout that triennium, so far as the LME was concerned, *the margin between the lowest and the highest prices* was only 15 per cent in 1961, down to 4 per cent in 1962 and a mere ONE per cent in 1963! One would assume that these were halcyon days for both copper producers and for the user-industrialists concerned.

In 1964, however, for some reasons unknown to the writer, the situation got out of hand and the LME price rose from a minimum of £236 to a maximum of £531 – by 125 per cent within that year. It does not seem necessary to pursue this matter further excepting to re-emphasize that under PSC auspices, as soon as reserves came to be held, *price movements on the LME would be closely in line with whatever was the statutorily prescribed price band for every metal that came to be held in PSC reserves.* And that these would generally average out at close to the Index level – of course plus handling costs and normal brokerage.

It is not overlooked that there is currently in existence an Organization termed the Inter-Government Consultative Council of Copper Exporting Countries (CIPEC) which comprises copper-mining interests in Chile, Peru, Zambia and Zaire – whence some 36 per cent of world copper production is derived. Whether or not CIPEC will later come to include the other major copper-mining countries is an open question. In any event it is to be kept in mind that copper is susceptible to substitution, e.g., by aluminium, and it would seem that copper producers the world over would welcome the inclusion of this metal within a PSC's scope.

D.8 CORRESPONDING SITUATIONS IN OTHER COMMODITY MARKETS. What occurs on the London Metal Exchange is mirrored in terminal markets concerned with other commodities – here epitomized:

Sugar: The volume of sugar imports in 1973 at 1,997,000 tons was greater than the quinquennial average (1969–73) by 34,000 tons at an average cost (cif) of £75 per ton, whereas during the preceding five years the average had been £58. But such imports were made up of much the greater part of those purchased under the Commonwealth Sugar Agreement at a negotiated price ranging from £42 to £50 per ton (described in Chapter 7) which accounted for some 1,600,000 tons, leaving only about 400,000 tons to be sold on the London Sugar Terminal Market which is concerned only with 'free' sugar. Yet prices on the LST Market during 1973 ranged from £87 in February to £152 in December. It is here to be remembered that in October 1963, in which year the average cost (cif) of sugar was £59.1 per ton, the LST Market price rose to £105. Then during the following year it fell below £25, and at one stage in 1967 *it was down to £12.3 a ton*. In 1973 the paper turnover on the LST Market aggregated 45.5 million tons! During the first eleven months of 1974 the LST Market price exceeded £650 a ton in October and fell to £450 in November. If the pattern of 1963 be repeated the fall in sugar costs in 1975–76 is anyone's guess.

Cocoa: Although the imports of cocoa at 93,500 tons in 1973 were only 600 tons (0.6 per cent) below the quinquennial (1969 to 1973) average at 94,100 tons at a mean cost (cif) of £135 per ton, its prices on the London Cocoa Terminal Market rose by 211 per cent, from £312 per ton in January to £970 in August. In the event, the volume of cocoa traded on the London Cocoa Terminal Market exceeded *nine and a half million tons* – about 100 times the volume actually imported. As a matter of interest, during 1965 the market price for this product dropped to £94 per ton! Up to the end of October 1974, fluctuations on the ICT Market ranged from a minimum of £459 in January to a maximum of £905 in October.

D.9 PSC'S 'GEARING' SELF-RECTIFYING.

(a) As emphasized earlier, the purpose of the proposed system is to eliminate all-too fallible human judgement always actuated by the profit motive. In contrast PSC's functioning is based upon – and operates in accord with – physical factors, without regard to profit. But, as physical factors – in terms of future outputs – are themselves unpredictable, it needs to be so geared as to cope with any situation that may arise. At the time of writing the fear is not of excess production of essential basics, but that the output of these may not be able to cope with ever-increasing demand. In this regard, what appears in the next chapter should surely prove reassuring. If, on the one hand, the *initial* Index (although based on preceding physical factors) proves too low to attract reserves of this or that commodity, it rises automatically as prescribed; and, if it proves too high and attracts too large accumulations, it automatically reduces in prescribed inverse ratio to such aggregations. In the former event a measure of capital and enterprise will be *attracted* to the production of commodities shown to be in short supply; and, conversely, a measure of capital and enterprise will tend gradually to be *diverted* away from the production of commodities manifestly in *excess* supply.

(b) In such circumstances, with PSC's functioning making evident the actual supply-demand situation in respect of each commodity conditionally valorized, something approaching a balance in outputs in the primary field would come about of itself – over the long term. Again to reiterate, the ability of producers to convert surpluses to then current commercial demand (at prices never less than the applicable low *point* level) into sterling by disposing of such surpluses to PSC would facilitate their acquiring *earned* liquidity with which to buy reciprocally. To the extent that this additional purchasing power was expended upon manufactures, the demand for raw materials (many if not all of which would come to be available at known prices from PSC's reserves) would correspondingly increase. The overall outcome would be a progressive improvement in living standards everywhere.

D.10 FOR THE INFORMATION OF THE CURIOUS. Subject to what was said in B.4 (a) as to weighting in respect of inflation, and to increased shipping costs, the measure of conceivable investment by a Price Stabilizing Corporation in acquiring a full year's reserves (at preceding rate of requirements) of all commodities within a Key Control of £1,200 million would be as tabulated below; that is on the preposterous assumption that it was required to purchase ten FULL-BLOCK-SERIES, i.e., ten BLOCKS of every commodity within its scope.

If the Key Control were set at a higher level – as it might well be to embrace the widest practicable range of commodities – all such hypothetical figures would need to be adjusted upwards *pro rata*.

Full BLOCK Series	Investment Cost at low *point*	Cumulative	Selling Value at HIGH *point*	Cumulative
1st	£108 million	£120 million	£132 million	£132 million
2nd*	£102.6 ,,	£234 ,,	£125.4 ,,	£257.4 ,,
3rd	£97.2 ,,	£342 ,,	£118.8 ,,	£376.2 ,,
4th	£91.8 ,,	£406 ,,	£112.2 ,,	£488.4 ,,
5th	£86.4 ,,	£502 ,,	£105.6 ,,	£594.0 ,,
6th	£81.0 ,,	£592 ,,	£99.0 ,,	£693.0 ,,
7th	£75.6 ,,	£676 ,,	£92.4 ,,	£785.4 ,,
8th	£70.2 ,,	£754 ,,	£85.8 ,,	£871.2 ,,
9th	£64.8 ,,	£826 ,,	£79.2 ,,	£950.4 ,,
10th	£59.4 ,,	£892 ,,	£72.6 ,,	£1,023.0 ,,

and so on to utter absurdity.

*PSC has the option (which it is unlikely to be required to exercise) to defer, for three years, payments for purchases in excess of first BLOCKS— as in B.10.

That the above illustrative figures savour of the ridiculous is no more absurd than that market prices should be permitted to fluctuate by hundreds per cent as the result of pure speculation on commodity markets.

D.11 ATTITUDES OF OTHER INDUSTRIALIZED NATIONS. In the event, as pinpointed in B.13, other highly industrialized nations would hardly be likely passively to watch a British PSC building up large reserves of essential commodities; because, while it would sell on demand not only to British but likewise to foreign buyers on equal terms, all such purchases would have to be in sterling – at 22.2 per cent above the price that PSC had paid for them. This matter is dealt with fully in

Chapter 6 wherein it is shown that, following Great Britain's adoption of this system, other great industrialized nations would not be slow to follow that example – just as Britain's initiation of the Gold Standard around 1840 soon resulted in *multi*national inauguration of that system. As shown in Chapter 6, a series of unilaterally established Price Stabilizing Corporations – though operating completely independently – would inevitably lead to *ultimate inter*national harmony in commodity prices; and to a corresponding harmony in external monetary values – in terms of essential basic commodities.

D.12 EFFECTS ON LOW-INCOME COUNTRIES.

(a) It is to the economic and political advantage of the generally affluent nations – and in many instances it is their inherent moral responsibility – to co-operate with Low-Income countries in assisting their peoples greatly to improve their living standards. Many such countries are endowed with great mineral, forestal and (actual or potential) pastoral, plantation and agricultural wealth – notably in Africa and South America; whereas the natural resources of others are more-or-less limited to perennial increments from the soil. Then there are the mainland Asian territories with many of their peoples highly skilled – with immense natural wealth of widely diversified types – where industrialization proceeds apace. *Their* problems relate chiefly to the growths of their populations which they are endeavouring to stem. However, improved agricultural techniques leading to noteworthy increases in grain yields – along with kindred factors – can give rise to hopes that they will be able to become self-sufficient in terms of basic food-stuffs in the not distant future. These matters are elaborated upon in Chapter 5.

(b) While the *direct* advantages that could accrue to Low-Income countries from the functioning of the proposed system might seem to be limited to producer-exporters of substances physically eligible for inclusion within its scope, the indirect benefits should be wide-spread. Such eligible commodities would include industrial metals, timbers, rubber, sugar, cocoa, coffee and animal and vegetable fibres; and it could be said in respect of all these that their producer-exporters have been sitting pretty during the latter half of 1973 – and that they are still 'in clover' in 1974. But the measure of resulting advantage to each such country is largely dependent upon its share in the equity of large foreign concerns in cases in which a great bulk of production results from investments from outside sources. It is patently desirable that as large a part of the equity in all such enterprises should be held domestically. And, if that is to be achieved, it is manifest that long-term loans on the most favourable possible terms should be increasingly forthcoming from the International Bank for Reconstruction and Development.

D.13 GENERAL UPLIFT IN LIVING STANDARDS.

(a) As Lord Kaldor observes, in the second paragraph of his Preface, an outstanding advantage of the proposed system is that it spreads the sources of money-making far and wide among the commodity-producers of the world – thereby generating and sustaining reciprocal purchasing power. And, as this expands – with consequential improvements in living standards – so does the demand for raw materials from which to process or fabricate the forms of merchandise the basic producers need. Thus, the expansion of primary production and of secondary (and tertiary) enterprises could result in something approaching near-balance as patterns of cause and (automatically regulating) effect.

(b) However, it is logical that Low-Income countries should wish to develop – or to expand – their own secondary industries; and this must become more evident in view of the inflation-engendered increase in costs of all the manufactures they import. Of course, in many regions it might seem that industrial expansion would necessitate very high tariff protection – at least initially; and once tariff walls are erected it takes something much more effective than Joshua's trumpet blasts to knock them down. Nevertheless it is to be kept in mind that in many lands industrial enterprises can have two real advantages: (i) raw materials at hand; and (ii) substantially lower money-wages than in predominantly industrialized communities; whereas the *real* values (as local buying-power) of such remunerations could be much greater than its money-value might indicate.

D.14 INTEREST OF INTERNATIONAL MONETARY AUTHORITIES EVOKED. It seems germane to mention here that, some time back, a representative of the International Bank for Reconstruction and Development – Mr Drugoslav Avramovic – came to see me, and we had a protracted discussion. His reactions encouraged me to believe that – with his great interest in and quick understanding of the principles of the system as it was explained to him – he came fully to appreciate that, under its aegis, the affording of essential finance by the IBRD to under-developed regions would be far more well-warranted (in the pure economic sense) than if commodity price fluctuations continued to be uncurbed. More recently (since this book was commenced) I had a visit from Mr Lal Jarawadena, who is representing Sri Lanka (formerly Ceylon), Pakistan and Bangladesh on the 'Group of Twenty' which is currently concerned with the problem of world monetary reform. We had a long talk as a result of which he manifestly came to understand the extent to which the stabilization of commodity prices would reflect upon the internal and external values of currencies. He subsequently wrote asking for copies of my Economic Research Council Paper (issued early in 1972 and of which this book is an updating and considerable elaboration) to distribute to his colleagues.

5. World Abundance Awaits Sane Development

E.1   THE GOOD EARTH. It is safe to assert that – jeremiads notwithstanding – there is no visible limit, and will not be in the foreseeable future, to the world's potential resources in those basic commodities that are the prime needs of men, at least in respect of perennial increments from the soil – and from the sea. Whereas that assertion needs some qualification in respect of mineral substances, it does not relate to potential supplies – which are illimitable – but to their accessibility.

E.2   NATURE DEMANDS INTELLIGENT CO-OPERATION. However, if nature is to yield a full measure of her bounty in perennial increments, she demands – from men the world-over – ever-increasing intelligent co-operation, taking such forms as: irrigation on the one hand, soil drainage on the other; better systems of cultivation, soil improvements by making good deficiencies in trace elements; the countering of erosion and the wide and wise use of fertilizers; the 'breeding' of new strains of cereals and other types of plant life – and of livestock – adapted to varying climatic conditions; pest and parasite control on the one hand and, on the other, capitalizing the valuable help afforded by various types of insects, as witness the elimination of the 'prickly pear' which (introduced from Mexico to Queensland by cacti devotees) 'escaped' into farmlands of which it took-over huge areas – defying every human effort to thwart its spreading. That is, until the cochineal beetle – which thrives on that sort of cactus – was brought in (from Spain). Within a few years, the 'prickly pear' had disappeared. Similarly, the introduction of myxomatosis put paid to the rabbit menace which had for long plagued the pastoral industry throughout south-eastern Australia.

E.3 IRRIGATION.

(a) In respect of irrigation there should be no curb put upon the imagination as to what can be contrived – given the capital essential to man's ingenuity being exercised to the full – whereby deserts can be transformed into veritable gardens. It is trite to assert that if a tenth of the capital and skill dissipated on armaments were devoted to irrigation projects, even to the extent (e.g.) of turning rivers inland instead of their pouring wastefully into the seas – thereby making arid regions fully productive – surely half that political conflict (and of all-too-well-warranted internal social discords) would vanish. As to changing the course of rivers, I cite one example of something that has been done during recent years in Australia. The Snowy River – fed from the vast seasonally snow-covered Australian Alps in southern New South Wales and flowing eastward into the Pacific – was dammed at a high level, establishing immense reservoirs, one of which extends over 33,000 acres to a depth of 300 feet, from which tens of miles of tunnels (of up to 15 feet diameter) were driven through solid rock to supplement the 1,500 mile west-flowing Murray River. And thereby millions of acres of potentially fruitful – but too often parched if not drought-stricken – land were brought under intensive cultivation. And, of course, full use is being made of the hydro-electric potential thus provided.

(b) Let us keep in mind other great and greater irrigation enterprises and projects – notably in the USA. In India, for example, three reservoirs – resulting from the damming of the rivers Bhakra, Krishna and Mahanandi – now impound a total of some 40 million acre-feet of water, equivalent to 30 inches of annual rainfall, applied when required to 15 million acres, in addition to natural but unreliable precipitation. It is not without interest that the area of England is less than $3\frac{1}{2}$ million acres and that our annual average rainfall is some 30 inches. In Egypt, the Aswan High Dam – completed in 1963 – is another striking example of what becomes practicable given the necessary capital and enterprise.

E.4 DESALINATION.

(a) Then there is the immeasurable factor in respect of the desalination of sea water for irrigation of which the potential (e.g.) on the hinterlands bordering the Mediterranean – and elsewhere – is limitless. It cannot be beyond the wit of men so to utilize concentrated solar heat as to distil vast volumes of sea water (and, in some localities, of brackish water which – as such – is inimical to plant life) to revitalize immense areas. There are other means, too, of desalting water (or eliminating brackish elements). In 1973 there were 330 desalting enterprises operating within the USA, for the most part treating brackish deposits. And many other such projects are in prospect in that country. Israel too is showing what can be done. With natural resources in 'fresh' form severely limited, expansion of agriculture in that country, where irrigation is essential, must depend on the results of desalination, in research on which many scientists are engaged. There are currently four different systems employed: the Zarchin freezing technique, the electrodialysis process, the reverse osmosis, and the flash evaporation methods. The Zarchin system is based on salt's separating from sea-water when it is frozen. Under electrodialysis process the water is desalinated by passing electric currents through the liquid and separating the salts thuswise. This is not the place in which to enter into technical details but these are set out in a booklet entitled *Economy* obtainable from Kater Publishing Ltd, PO Box 7145, Jerusalem.

(b) Apropos the elimination of salt with the freezing of sea-water, there was a suggestion seemingly under serious consideration a few years back in Australia which involved the towing of huge icebergs from the Antarctic to irrigate arid lands bordering the Great Australian Bight! Absurd as this may seem, it would have been regarded as fantastic nonsense, when I was a boy, that a mere whisper in Melbourne would come to be heard in London – and the very acme of folly to have suggested that one would live to see men walking on the moon.

E.5 UTILIZATION OF SOLAR HEAT.
(a) It would seem that the harnessing of solar heat could be a prime source from which to derive much of that energy which is in increasing demand. For irrigation of arid lands adjacent to the sea in hot climates, one visualizes large concave mirrors automatically geared so as to concentrate intense heat

(in turn) on a series of large iron boilers. These could be set below sea-level to be gravitationally pipe-fed; and there should be no great problem involved in distilling the resulting constant flow of steam generated during sunlit hours. Such installations would require considerable capital outlay; but, once installed, their operating costs would be negligible. Their 'raw materials' – sea-water and solar rays – are inexhaustible, and *there would be no resulting pollution*! Perhaps someone may commend this notion to the wealth-encumbered Oil Sheiks.

(b) Opportunely enough, since I started this chapter, there came through my letter-box a copy of 'Radio Australia News' (1.5.74) with an item headed *Wide Interest in New Solar Energy Device* which reads: 'Interest has been shown by Australian and overseas companies in a new solar energy device invented by three Tasmanian scientists – Dr M. D. Waterworth, Dr R. C. McFadyean and Mr T. J. Wilson. It is called a deflection grating – a small, mirror-like object that disperses light much as does a prism . . . and absorbs solar energy more effectively than any existing device.'

E.6 NUCLEAR-POWER-ENGENDERED HEAT. As to what could be achieved by the usage of thermo-nuclear heat in the distillation of sea-water, it would seem that, technically, there is no limit. The initial installation cost may appear today to be out of all proportion to the value of the results – but techniques improve with consequent economies.

E.7 ARTIFICIAL FERTILIZERS. More needs to be said as to the highly important matter of adequate supplies of artificial fertilizers, the production of which demands considerable capital outlay. Professor George Allen (of the University of Aberdeen) recently estimated that the world shortage in 1974 is some $3\frac{1}{2}$ million tons, chiefly of nitrogenous elements the production of which is an expensive process; the more so because of the rise in costs of petroleum which is its prime derivative. Yet it is in the ill-developed countries that such fertilizers are most essential. A few years back the so-called 'Green Revolution' in India encouraged predictions that that country could be transformed from being a considerable importer of wheat into a consistent exporter of that grain; but such expansion of production depends almost wholly upon ample supplies of nitrogenous fertilizers – and India is just unable to pay prices that would prove profitable to commercial enterprise. Hence this is surely a matter which should have unstinted support from the International Bank for Reconstruction and Development.

E.8   LEGUMES.   There is, of course, another – and natural – means of similarly endowing soils via legumes which are nitrogen-fixing. It should perhaps be explained that a legume is a type of plant which, of high protein content and therefore valuable as stock-feed, harbours nitrogen in its roots – depositing this in the soil to the advantage of other vegetation. Typical examples, generally with pulse-like seeds, are peas and beans (especially soya, of which more appears in E.22), lucerne (alfalfa) and most of the clovers – particularly subterranean clover notably in soils aided by super-phosphate fertilizer. The problem is to find types of legume which will survive in dry climates – something that adds to the importance of constantly increasing areas under irrigation.

E.9   PASTORAL PRODUCTION.   While the foregoing has special applicability to agricultural and plantation enterprises, many of the requirements set out above extend also into pastoral fields in the world-wide open spaces – whereon there are other special requirements essential for the well-being of livestock. Such measures include: artesian bores, deep earth tanks – plastic-lined to prevent soakage-loss, and maybe plastic-covered (with this material slightly quilted to ensure buoyancy) to counteract evaporation which in some tropical areas reduces exposed water-surfaces by up to seven feet within the year! There is also the need to dam streams which, though raging torrents under monsoonal rains, rapidly degenerate into occasional waterholes. Moreover, if the best results are to be achieved, water so conserved needs to be taken to well-distributed drinking troughs (via plastic piping), necessitating windmills or other pumping devices to elevated water-tanks; because, in dry periods, the grazing area is limited to the distance livestock can move daily from their drinking places. Other essentials are conservation of fodder (harvested following the luscious growth during good seasons) and the economic use of pasture by sub-divisional fencing with the enclosed areas used in rotation.

E.10 REMUNERATION FACTORS. All such measures are forms of increasingly intelligent co-operation with nature, and they are so detailed to emphasize that the producer (always having to cope with natural hazards) has to invest many years of work and heavy capital outlay before he obtains the fruits of his labour and investment. And, unless he has positive assurances as to the minimum prices he will receive for his products, he is groping in the dark – gambling with the unpredictable – always with recollections of the tragic breakdown of the price structure during the twenties and thirties – something that was emphasized in my opening chapter. And there is this to be added: with ever-growing urbanization in industrialized nations the vast majority of people thus involved have drifted so far from primary production that it is as well that they should be reminded of their constant dependence for the essentials of life upon those who till the soil, tend the flocks and herds, fish the seas, range the forests and prise mineral wealth from the earth.

E.11 FISH-FARMING. Although a PSC would not be concerned with fish (except *possibly* in durably-preserved form – vide B.23), it is germane to the context of this chapter to refer to the important matter of fish-farming as witness our own trout-hatcheries. This sort of enterprise has long been practised (particularly in China) in respect of fresh-water fishes; and it is now being similarly applied to sea-fish – notably in some Scottish lochs. Such enterprises could go far to compensate not only for exploitation by trawlers but also to counteract normal depredations upon what are initially prolific regenerations; and the same sort of 'farming' can be increasingly applied to many molluscs as well as to turtles, of which only a tiny proportion reach the haven of the sea after being incubated. And turtle soup is delectable fare as, indeed, is turtle meat.

E.12 IRONICAL INCIDENCE. Reverting to the rural producer, it has long been the quintessence of irony that if there be a widespread good season – or series of good seasons – markets almost invariably collapse; this notwithstanding that a possible preceding bad season had caused prices to soar, much to the disadvantage of the consumer. In short, it is to the mutual interest of primary producers, of legitimate intermediaries (as distinct from mere speculators) and ultimate consumers that there should be continuity of supply at realistically stable prices – something that has not thus far been achieved but which, as made evident in this book, is surely attainable – although the process must inevitably be gradual.

E.13 GRAINS. Grains are outstandingly the most important of man's needs. Of course, there still remain such primitives as dwell in remote regions in South America and in Africa, who know not agriculture and who have no domestic livestock. But, these people apart, grains are the staple diet of men: wheat so far as Europeans – and an increasing proportion of other peoples – are concerned; and, for the rest, rice, maize, sorghum and other cereals.

E.14 WHEAT.

(a) Let us first consider wheat, the cost of which strongly influences that of all other grains, including feeding-stuffs for livestock and its cost-effects on prices of food-stuffs derived from animals so fed. As will be shown in G.5 of Chapter 7, the strange activities of the United States Commodity Credit Corporation, with its progressively rising price support policy for wheat (and for other commodities) in post-war years were demonstrably primarily responsible for the onset of serious inflation, not only within the United States of America but literally throughout the Western World.

(b) *Significance of Wheat Costs:* Around the turn of the century one often heard the dictum '*When wheat is a dollar a bushel all's well in the world*'. That was at a period when men trudged after horse-drawn ploughs (I write from personal experience prior to 1914), maybe turning over two or three furrows, when the wheat had to be reaped at ground level, bound into sheaves and hand-stooked to dry out (if it did not inopportunely rain heavily – when the grain would commence sprouting in the stooks) before being put into carefully thatched stacks to await the arrival of threshing and winnowing machines, whereupon the stack was pulled to pieces to be pitchforked through these processes. But we ultimately got the wheat! It was when that was the order of affairs that the *'dollar a bushel wheat'* dictum was proclaimed. Thereafter the mechanization of wheat production so developed that one man was able annually to plough, cultivate, sow and harvest around 500 acres singlehanded; and, thanks to soil improvement and other forms of good management, wheat yields per acre increased markedly, often to double – sometimes to treble – what had been produced in the nineteenth century. Of course, large-scale cultivation requires considerable capital outlay on tractors and cultivating and harvesting equipment – at constantly increasing cost. And, at time of writing, there is a lot of uncertainty as to continuity of supply of fuel oil and its cost.

(c) *Principal Exporters:* The chief wheat exporting countries in the 'new' world are the United States, Canada, Australia and Argentina, in none of which countries were agricultural activities disrupted by actual hostilities within their mainland boundaries during either the First or Second World Wars; whereas agriculture was brought to a standstill over vast areas of Europe including Russia in Europe and (in the second great conflict) in Asia.

(d) *Wartime Expansion:* So it was that – especially during the Second World War – maximum acreages were sown and output gathered increasing momentum in North America and Australia. However, the rapidity of post-war recovery in agricultural outputs in what had been the devastated regions of Europe was indeed noteworthy. For example, during 1952 the USSR was already an exporter of wheat, with the United Kingdom receiving 451,549 tons; and such exports from Russia continued until 1962 – with an annual average exceeding 451,000 tons.

(e) *Post-war Surpluses:* In these circumstances vast stocks in North America (with the US CCC holding 37 million tons in sterile hoard in the early fifties) were virtually unsaleable; and there were large surplus stocks also in Canada and – from time to time – in Australia. That situation persisted for several years until poor seasons in the USSR (which, be it repeated, had been previously a consistent exporter of this grain) and virtual famine in China led to large consignments to these countries from both Canada and Australia – truly a case of one man's poison being another man's *wheat*! But, for strategic-cum-political reasons, the USA stood aloof until it commenced to export to Russia in 1971, and to China in 1973. In the first eight months of the latter year American consignments to Russia reached nearly eight million tons, and to China over a million – an aggregate of some nine million tons. It was then (in what appeared to be a world wheat shortage situation) that quick-buck-making speculators entered the lists – with chaotic results not only in the US but elsewhere.

(f) *A Three-hundred-per-cent Increase in Wheat Prices:* In the event, the costs (cif) of wheat in the United Kingdom (average of 'soft' and 'hard' types) which had been close to £27 a ton in the quinquennium 1964–68 rose to an average of £34 during the succeeding five years – with market prices in Britain, in late 1973 and 1974, ranging from £51.00 to £104.90 for 'hard' wheat (representing practically the whole of her imports from North America) and from £37.50 to £66.75 for 'soft' wheat – with devastating consequences on food costs; and, with so much more high-priced wheat in the pipeline, scant prospect of these reducing in the early future. *So what of that future?*

(g) *Payments for NOT Sowing Wheat in USA:* It is here to be noted that the maximum area sown to wheat in the US was 84 million acres for the 1959–60 season, whereas during the 1972–73 season the area so planted had fallen to 55 million acres – a reduction of 29 million acres. This (as the average yield per acre in that year was 32.8 bushels) meant that the potential output from the USA in that season was lower by 948 million bushels (some 25 million tons) than it would have been if the preceding maximum area had in fact been harvested with corresponding levels of yields. In this connection American farmers in the 1972–73 season were *actually paid $27 an acre* (by the US Commodity Credit Corporation) *NOT to plant wheat on 21 million acres* previously devoted to that grain – at a cost to the American taxpayer of $567 million. It is to be noted that, while US market prices had remained close to $63 (around £26) per long ton for some years up to mid-1972, they then commenced a sudden upward surge which by February

1974 had reached a monthly average of $222 (around £93) per ton.

(h) *Canadian and Australian Potentials:* Turning now to Canada, the maximum area ever sown to wheat in that country was 30 million acres in the 1967–68 season; whereas for the 1972–73 season it was reduced to 21 million acres, which, as the yield was 25 bushels to the acre, represented a reduction from what might have been produced – *if the preceding acreage had been sown* – of 225 million bushels (six million tons). In respect of Australia, the maximum sown at 27 million acres was in 1968–69; while, for the 1972–73 season, it was 18.5 million acres, which, as the yield in 1972–73 was only 13 bushels to the acre, represented a reduction from what might have been produced – *if the proven maximum acreage had been sown* – of 110 million bushels (3 million tons). Actually it had been a very poor season in Australia, where the 13 bushels per acre was far below the average yield, which usually stands at from 16 to 20 bushels and more to the acre.

E.15 WHEAT SITUATION SUMMARIZED.

(a) Thus the *proven* output capacity of these three nations was as shown in the following table:

	Maximum Acreage Ever Sown	Gross Yield	Compared with 1972–73				
			Area Sown	Yield per acre	Gross Yield	Reductions in areas sown	Probable loss in outputs
	Million acres	Million tons	Million acres	Bushels	Million tons	Million acres	Million tons
USA	84 (49–50)	30	55.0	32.8	42.0	29.0	25
Canada	30 (67–68)	16	21.0	25.0	14.5	9.0	6
Australia	27 (68–69)	15	18.5	13.0	6.5	8.5	3
Totals	141	61	94.5		63.0	46.5	34

(b) When the 'loss' in potential yield of 34 million tons be added to the unexpectedly high exports at close to *nine million tons* to the Communist countries, we arrive at an aggregate of nearly 43 million tons. It is here to be noted that the harvest in the USSR in 1974 is reported to have been an all-time record not only of wheat but also of other grains. However, in view of Russia's experience in recent years, it would seem unlikely that she would export much of any grain surplus to her current needs. It is far more probable that, in the light of recent experiences, any such excess would be put into reserve.

(c) That immense additional areas could be sown to wheat in North America and Australia is not open to question; and the potential for increasing outputs in South America (especially in Argentina) as well as in the other continents is beyond dispute. Moreover, it is just as likely that Russia will enjoy bountiful seasons, as in 1974, as it is that unfavourable weather conditions should recur as in some earlier years.

E.16 INDIA AND CHINA.

(a) In respect of India the best that can be hoped for is that the optimism that has been expressed in regard to the projected 'Green Revolution' referred to in E.7 will be enabled to materialize in the near future; and that, in the meantime, India may be favoured with at least occasional bountiful seasons.

(b) As to China, the data are just not available regarding the current or future potential situation in respect of wheat production. But we are all aware that it is the determined policy of this great nation with its 800 million people to become self-supporting as soon as may be in all essential commodities; and – whether one agrees or disagrees with the political system there in operation – there is abundant evidence that its goal will be achieved. Of course, seasonal factors will always obtain, but the Chinese are bent upon combating these with ever-expanding irrigation and/or drainage schemes as applicable, plus, of course, soil improvement and other essential advances in techniques.

E.17 THE INTERNATIONAL WHEAT COUNCIL.

(a) To what extent, it may well be asked, has the functioning of the International Wheat Council figured in respect of this grain over the past decade? It is certainly not to denigrate the value of this organization's work to assert that from the signing of the first post-war International Wheat Agreement (to cover the four years 1949–53 inclusive) its functioning has been fraught with difficulties. Suffice it to say here that it was certainly due to IWC's influence that imported wheat prices were held steady for a number of years until 1973; but at what this writer believes to have been too high levels for reasons explained in Chapter 7.

(b) However, it would seem germane to mention here that if

it had not been for the disruptive activities of the US Commodity Credit Corporation – that is if the International Wheat Agreement of 1949 had been permitted unimpededly to operate – the price per bushel of wheat by 1953 would probably have been stabilized (i.e., from $1.30 to $1.60) at around $1.45 (fob port of despatch) with an absolute maximum of $1.80 and a not improbable minimum of $1.20 a bushel; a likely average of $55.50 per ton – equivalent in the early fifties to around £20 per ton. And that order of affairs could have been subsequently maintained for a decade if not for very much longer; or *it could have been if it had been within the authority of the IWC to establish reserves* which unfortunately was something outside its scope.

E.18 PROSPECT OF PSC ACQUIRING RESERVES OF WHEAT.
(a) In the ordinary way it could confidently be anticipated that the phenomenally high prices for wheat in late 1973 and 1974 would result in maximum areas being sown for the 1974–75 season; and the overall result could be a world-wide surplus, not perhaps above the real needs of men but in terms of remunerative prices. But (as has been said) growers in the chief wheat-exporting nations will surely have in mind the acute slump conditions of the late twenties and early thirties; and, within the USA, political pressures are likely to result in the US CCC support price again being increased. And, as the USA is the major exporter of this grain, the reflex action would seem likely more-or-less (relatively) to increase prices so far as Canada, Australia, and Argentina are concerned, both domestically and for export. However, all factors considered, there is certainly a possibility (if not a probability sooner or later) of world wheat outputs being far in excess of (then) effective demand, even at around the average of prices throughout the quinquennium 1969–73 – and certainly dismissing as absurd those obtaining during 1974.

(b) It would be at such a stage that a British Price Stabilizing Corporation, with its *initial* wheat Index and *points* at realistic levels, might well be called upon to buy and thus to establish reserves of this most important of food-stuffs. It must surely be obvious that there is no alternative means of engendering confidence among wheat-growers who can increase or reduce their annual sowings at will.

E.19 OIL CRISIS EFFECTS ON PRODUCTION COSTS – AND FREIGHTS.

(a) Of course the major factor in recent increases in prices – on all sides – has been the oil crisis of November 1973, pregnant as it was with uncertainties, of which some have since lessened. In regard to all forms of agriculture depending on oil-derived energy, farmers have serious fears, as to both the quantities of oil they will be able to obtain and as to its costs. Moreover, such misgivings were enhanced (as were those of importing countries) by the inevitable increase in freight charges and probable restrictions in available cargo space – forebodings all-too-well warranted.

(b) For wheat imported to Britain from North America, average shipping rates (from Gulf Ports) rose from £3.40 per long ton during 1971–72 to £8.79 in the following year, and to £17.59 over the first quarter of 1974; and the corresponding average of increases in freights from Australia (Eastern States) were from £5.21 (1971–72) to £8.79 (1972–73) and up to £17.75 in the first quarter of 1974. However, at time of writing, it may be expected that the oil situation will improve, in which connexion attention is invited to E.29 and E.31 later in this chapter.

E.20 BRITISH INTERNAL SITUATION. Dependent to the extent that Britain is on imported wheat, the situation arising from exaggerated predictions as to world shortages of this (and other) grains has been indeed unfortunate.

(b) In this context, particular interest attaches to a statement, recently televised by the BBC, by Mr Travers Legge – Editor of *Farmers' Weekly* – who confidently stated that the United Kingdom could produce its own full wheat-requirements. After hearing this I asked him if he meant that we could grow enough not only for human consumption of breadstuffs but also sufficient for livestock. He replied that both such requirements could be met, given wiser utilization of our land – but with the qualification that it would have to be of 'soft' types. While Mr Legge's opinion may be disputed, there would seem to be no doubt that domestic output of this grain could be substantially increased. Personally, I have always been puzzled by British millers' (and bakers') insistence that 'hard' wheats are essential for making bread to the taste of domestic consumers. This may be something of a myth (and Mr Legge shares that view) because in France practically all milling is of 'soft' types – and I have yet to hear anyone question the excellence of French bread.

E.21 OTHER GRAINS.

(a) So far as barley, oats and rye are concerned, it will suffice to say that generally speaking each will thrive wherever wheat can be successfully cultivated. In contrast, maize and sorghum require heavy and regular rainfall (or irrigation) and a warm climate if they are to prosper. And of course rice is cultivated in what are virtually swamp conditions during stages of its growth. That outputs of all these cereals can be immeasurably increased, in these several parts of the world that are climatically propitious, is surely beyond dispute.

(b) *Triticale.* A notable example of the way in which man's ingenuity has been harnessed to increase world food output is the development of a wheat-hybrid called triticale – a cross between rye and wheat. Its advantages are that it combines rye's adaptability to unfavourable environmental conditions, such as cold weather and light sandy or acid soils (where rye may flourish), with the high yield of wheat which requires more favourable conditions. In addition the more advanced types of this hybrid are proving more resistant to the menace of 'rust' to which wheat is subject. Triticale is now being grown over more than a million acres in 52 countries, ranging from the Prairies of Canada to the foothills of the Himalayas. In Ethiopia and India it has already outyielded wheat, while in Mexico the best varieties are now exceeding the highest wheat outputs (both summer and winter) by over 15 per cent. It would seem that, as triticale has a greater adaptability than either of its 'parents', it becomes possible to grow a high protein crop in what are termed 'marginal lands'. The resulting 'flour' has virtually the same utility and nutritional values as wheat-flour. Furthermore it would seem that triticale's straw may prove a good forage crop for cattle. Overall, the objective is to provide more food for people who depend mainly on grains for their sustenance.

E.22 SOYA BEANS.

(a) Much has been heard in recent years about the soya bean. Originating in China, its cultivation on a commercial scale elsewhere – especially in the USA – is a comparatively recent development. It was first sown experimentally by the Americans in the thirties when wheat was in huge surplus; and, over the intervening decades, so diversely valuable did this bean prove to be that 56 million acres were sown in that country for the 1973 harvest, in which year its exports of soya were valued at $3,000 million.

(b) The utility values of this bean are perhaps greater than that of any other vegetable product; and given favourable climatic conditions (good rainfall – *or irrigation* – and hottish weather in the initial growing period) it will flourish in any of the continents. It happens that, in 1945, I secured a small supply which I sowed in Buckinghamshire. I do not recall the climatic conditions in that summer, but those beans thrived exceedingly with a good yield which, picked before they had hardened and as though they were ordinary green peas, were excellent.

(c) The special merit of the soya is its richness in protein content (and it has the additional advantage of being one of the valuable legumes referred to earlier). It has a high oil and fat content and is now a major ingredient in margarine – which in the USA has displaced butter by a ratio of two to one as compared with a ratio in reverse of seven to one in 1940. It is increasingly replacing meat as a substitute and as an additive – as in sausages. It can be so processed as even to provide 'milk' which is said to be as nutritious as that from cows. The residues – or the crushed beans themselves – are uniquely valuable as stock-feed – particularly for milch cows and calves, pigs and poultry.

(d) Following much study by botanical biologists in the USA, new varieties have been developed suitable for cultivation under varying climatic conditions and on different types of soil; and yields have been steadily increased. Other countries have benefited from this work, notably Mexico, Brazil and India. According to Mr Folke Dovering, writing in *The Scientific American*, the results are particularly encouraging in India where some of the US strains have produced higher yields than they do within America. Manifestly the potential for great increases in outputs of this uniquely valuable pulse is highly promising. In short, it has provided what might well be termed a new dimension in agricultural economics.

E.23 SUGAR.

(a) The sources from which this product is derived commercially are sugar-cane, requiring a tropical climate, and sugar-beet which will thrive in any temperate zone where there are reliable seasonal rains; and which, as an annual crop, provides a useful rotation with cereals. But the fact outstands that neither in Britain nor in any other developed country could beet-sugar be produced excepting with government subsidy – along with tariff protection. In striking contrast, cane-sugar, which can be cultivated to produce vast quantities in areas favoured by adequate rainfalls and a hot climate, requires no subsidy but only a realistically remunerative stable price. Those of us who recall conditions during both World Wars have vivid recollections of the acute sugar shortages during and following those periods – and it was such situations which strongly encouraged its domestic production in Britain and the rest of Europe. And, once European farmers come by a boon, they are naturally averse from its being discontinued.

(b) The major sugar-cane producers are Cuba – and other West Indian islands – Mauritius, Fiji, Australia, India and Brazil as well as many South American, Asian and African territories which, *in toto*, represent an immeasurable potential for increased output. But whereas sugar-beet is an annual crop, sugar-cane (although it matures in between a year and two years) will grow again after being cut and can be re-harvested for several years in succession – a process termed ratooning. References have earlier been made to the vicissitudes through which the sugar industry has passed with its post-war prices ranging from as catastrophically low as £12.3 per ton in 1963 to over £650 in 1974 on the London Terminal Sugar Market! While beet-growers were safeguarded, as were those cane-growers whose interests were protected (up to a point) under the Commonwealth Sugar Agreement, other cane-growers had no sort of protection – the efforts of the International Sugar Organization notwithstanding. Further reference is made to the operations of both the Commonwealth Sugar Exporters Association and the International Sugar

Organization in Chapter 7. Suffice it to say here that there would appear to be no visible limit to the volume of cane-sugar that could be produced in suitable tropical regions. That sugar can be held in store indefinitely is not open to question.

(c) In terms of refined sugar, while the average yield per acre from beet is about 2 tons, from cane it is 50 per cent higher at above *three* tons. Moreover, whereas the European farmer has the alternative of growing grains and other crops, along with livestock enterprises – with markets virtually at his gate – the cane grower has no corresponding alternative enterprises to which he can have recourse for export.

E.24 COCOA.

(a) Cocoa is derived from the seed of the cacao tree native to South America, which has been introduced to many other countries. It requires rich, well-watered soil, heavy rainfall, high humidity and a constant high temperature if it is to thrive. Grown from seed, it takes about five years to come into bearing. The main sources of supply – all developing countries – are Ghana, Nigeria and other West African territories, though it is cultivated also in the Pacific Islands and elsewhere. Depending on the type grown, full production is not attained until from seven to twelve years – according to varieties. The trees – with some seven hundred to the acre – require cultivation, spraying, pruning and so on. The average yield is about 400 lb per acre. Clearly, if cocoa producers are substantially to increase their outputs, and the areas in various parts of the world in which the required climatic conditions obtain are vast, they must have thus far-absent assurances that, following their years of work and capital outlay, they will receive continuity of remunerative prices. Inasmuch as the potential output is increased, so is the potential market for this highly nutritive product.

(b) The wide oscillation in prices of cocoa (from £312 to £970 a ton in the five years 1969–73) is highly disconcerting to the whole economies of such territories as Ghana whence cocoa is the main export – in which connection it may be mentioned that at one stage during 1965 the market price dropped to £94 a ton; and such fluctuations are of course equally disconcerting to user industries.

(c) While the cocoa bean is apt to deteriorate if kept for long periods in a humid climate – such as in West Africa – it can be held for years without appreciable deterioration in properly constructed stores in Great Britain.

E.25 COFFEE. Coffee like cocoa is derived from a bean-yielding tree cultivated plantation-wise in many territories having a warm moist climate. It thrives best around an elevation of 2,000 ft though differing types adapt to varying altitudes. Again like cocoa some five years elapse before trees come into bearing with output increasing as they mature.

This product is of special significance in respect of *world economy*. Petroleum apart, it involves greater money turnover than any other single commodity being traded internationally, with an annual value in 1973 of more than £1,747 million. Moreover coffee most clearly mirrors the division of the world into two distinct economic groups; the exporters all being developing – and almost all the importing-nations coming into the category of developed countries. It is to many producing territories an essential factor in their economic systems as it provides employment for more than 20 million people in over 40 producing regions. It is the source of 20 per cent or more of the foreign currency of six Latin American and nine African countries.

Coffee is a very important factor also in the economy of the United Kingdom, which in 1973 imported over 137,000 tons at an average cif price of £504 per ton. Its total cost at over £77 million was equivalent to about half that paid for wheat imports in the same year.

That the output of coffee could be vastly increased is beyond dispute. In fact, the world shortage in 1973–74 would appear to have been directly attributable to the destruction of large areas of plantations in Brazil – destructions resulting from falls in producers' receipts which had indicated that this product was in surplus supply. In the event as will be seen in the section dealing with the current International Coffee Agreement, Chapter 7 (G.9(b)), one of its provisions *defines maximum quotas* which producer-countries are *permitted* to export.

As under proper storage conditions coffee can be held in bean form indefinitely – without significant deterioration – it is unquestionably physically eligible to be brought within a

PSC's scope. Manifestly, under such auspices it is incredible that there would hardly be likely to be any limitation imposed on growers as to the volumes they were free to export.

E.26 RUBBER. As in the case of cacao – from the seeds of which cocoa is derived – the tree yielding latex (which when coagulated results in the elastic substance rubber) originated in South America, whence it was introduced to Malaya around 1890. Like cocoa it requires rich, well-watered soil, heavy rainfall, high humidity and a constant high temperature. It is now cultivated extensively not only in Malaya, but in Ceylon, Indonesia, Burma, Thailand and other South East Asian regions, as well as in Nigeria and other parts of West Africa. And there are vast additional areas where it thrives. However, the establishment of new – or the expansion of existing – plantations involves heavy capital outlay and a lapse of from five to seven years before full production is attained. It is enough for the planter to have to cope with natural hazards without his whole enterprise being reduced to the gamble implicit in the grossly unfair fluctuations in prices to which this product has been subjected. These have oscillated to a fantastic extent. In 1946 rubber was down to £18 per ton – when it was used as paving in Lombard Street in the City of London. In 1951 it rose to £163; in 1953 it fell back to £36. During the quinquennium 1970–74 (inclusive) its price on the London Terminal Market ranged from £128 in 1971 to £570 in January 1974, only to fall to £218 in November of that year. All rubber-growing areas are in developing countries.

At one stage it was considered likely that the natural substance would gradually be replaced by synthetic rubber – *derived from petroleum*; but, in the event, the demand for both types constantly increased. Manifestly, if rubber producers are to be expected to expand their plantations, they must have some assurance as to the minimum price they will receive when their additional trees come into production.

E.27 TIMBER. Wood – in a wide range of types, shapes and sizes down to wood-pulp – looms large in Britain's import bill – with its gross cif cost over the quinquennium 1970 to 1974 (inclusive) ranging from £430 million in 1970 to over £800 million in 1974. Its cost has in fact risen progressively from year to year, especially during 1973–74; and, excepting to the extent that the exploitation of natural (or man-planted) forests is offset by maturing timber-plantations, *it is a wasting asset.*

Although in certain standard shapes – or in pulp – which *might* be brought within PSC's scope, it is not suggested that it should be among the commodities *initially* included within a Price Stabilizing Corporation's range. In any event, it is highly questionable that its costs (cif) will drop by 10 per cent below the preceding quinquennial average in the foreseeable future.

However, two observations are here called for:

(i) *Afforestation:* So far as the UK (and, if one may so suggest, the Irish Republic) is (are) concerned the maximum possible area (that is of lands not used for pasture and/or cultivations – although such acreages can and ought to be greatly increased) should be planted with trees – both conifers and hardwoods. Abandoned railway tracks, totalling tens of thousands of acres – are immediately available (as are many roadsides); as well as great areas of moorlands and fells. One is aware that the planting of 'regiments' of conifers in these localities is rather frowned upon by some environmentalists; but the best of these are also conservationists. And afforestation is the acme of practical conservation with a vastly different result from activities resulting in pollution – an outstanding bane, not only of keen environmentalists but of us all.

(ii) *Deplorable Prolificacy:* The waste of timber, especially in the form of paper – from newsprint to cardboard packaging – is a shameful squandering of nature's bounty. Ironically it costs ratepayers vast sums for the collection, transport and destruction of *so-called* waste paper, whereas perhaps 80 per cent or more of that which is disposed of as garbage could be re-cycled – much of it for re-use as newsprint, and the rest for packaging or as an ingredient in such products as hardboard. And let it here be said that it is long over-time that the mania for packaging should be curbed. Every establishment, from offices or factories to domestic household, should be provided by Local Authorities with receptacles for *discarded* paper; and it should be an offence to put other than dirty paper in garbage tins.

E.28 ILLIMITABLE MINERAL RESERVES AWAIT EXPLOITATION.
Turning now to mineral substances of all types, it is incontestable that – though in a sense markedly different from perennial increments from the soil – there is no limit in terms of volumes to their availability, given the capital, enterprise and advanced techniques essential to their exploitation. As to industrial metals, the importance of their being re-cycled to a maximum practicable extent cannot be too strongly stressed.

E.29 PETROLEUM.
(a) The action of the Organization of Petroleum Exporters in reducing their outputs and increasing their prices in late 1973 was widespread in its unfortunate consequences – but surely only for the time being. One result has been a remarkable reduction in oil consumption, a matter that has recently been investigated by the Washington Energy Co-ordination Group. During the last week of June 1974 this consortium of twelve nations issued a report estimating that during the second half of 1974 there would have been a *daily* surplus of 1.5 million barrels which would rise to 2.7 million barrels a day in the first half of 1975. Such a *volte face* from the earlier gloomy predictions is as unexpected as it is bewildering to the uninitiated in this sphere. However, looking back to the action taken by OPEC in late 1973, something of that sort was not altogether surprising in view of the extent to which the economies of the countries comprising that organization are dependent on oil exports – and a recognition of their latent power in these respects had been an added spur to exploration, especially off-shores, in various parts of the globe.

(b) A mere ten years ago who could have foreseen that vast oil deposits would be discovered under the North Sea; or that, from being an importer of the whole of its petroleum needs, Australia – within a decade – would be producing more than half its oil requirements as a result of its offshore drilling; with the prospect of being self-sufficient in this respect in the foreseeable future. In short, the potential supply of oil in liquid form is beyond estimation; and, of course, there are other sources from which it can be obtained, notably coal, shale and tar-sands. The deposits of black coal in Britain and in many other parts of the world are likewise beyond estimation. The same is true of shale, which has world-wide distribution with particularly large deposits in the USA, in which respect it was recently stated during a BBC documentary that there is more oil in Colorado shale than all that has yet been derived from drilled wells in the United States. As to tar-sands, those in the Canadian State of Alberta are estimated to contain some 14,000 million tons of petroleum. The cost of its extraction from such sources is, of course, another matter, but against this must be offset constantly improving techniques with resulting economies.

E.30 INDUSTRIAL METALS.

(a) **Iron ore:** As to metals, I again instance Australia – simply because I happen to be rather more familiar with what has happened in that country than elsewhere. In 1960 I was afforded facilities to travel widely in my native land, from which I had been absent for some thirty-five years, to get the data for my book *Australia in the 1960's*. At that time, the proved reserves (in official parlance 'demonstrated reserves') of high grade iron ore (of 50 per cent or greater ferrous content) were given at 318 million tons; and its export was prohibited excepting under official licence. Within the next five years the proved reserves of such ore had risen to 29,000 million tons!

(b) **Bauxite:** Prior to 1955, the Australians – not having found any bauxite of other than low grade – were importing this substance from Jamaica for their single aluminium-making installation at Bell Bay in Tasmania. But in that year enormous deposits of high grade bauxite were discovered at Weipa on the western side of Cape York Peninsula, to be followed by further discoveries in Arnhem Land on the opposite side of that Gulf, as well as in other parts of the Northern Territory (of which Arnhem Land is a part) and also in Western Australia. Thus, within twenty years, that island continent has become one of the greatest producers of this substance.

(c) **Copper:** As to copper, around 1950, the proved reserves of copper in ore within Australia and adjacent Papua aggregated 517,000 tons. In contrast, within 1972, the output from one mine (Mount Isa in Western Queensland) exceeded 150,000 tons, and that in Bougainville (an island off Papua) 180,000 tons. And several other mines were then producing considerable quantities of this metal.

These are only three of the many examples that might be cited of newly discovered mineral wealth in one or other – or all – of the five continents.

E.31 RUNNING OUT OF MINERAL SUPPLIES. . . . 'RIDICULOUS'. Overall it may suffice to quote certain excerpts from an Official Paper issued by the Canadian Department of Energy, Mines and Resources in January 1973, prepared by the eminent mineralogist, Mr David E. Brooks, who writes:

In literal terms, the notion of running out of mineral supplies is ridiculous. The entire planet is composed of minerals, and man can hardly mine himself out, though one of the most amusing applications of exponential growth curves indicates that if sand and gravel production continue to expand at rates typical of the past 20 years, the whole earth will soon be consumed.

Specifically, except for a few substances, notably crude oil and natural gas, which are discretely different from the rock masses that contain them, the quantities of mineral materials in even the upper few miles of the earth's crust approach the infinite. A single cubic mile of average crustal rock contains a billion tons of aluminium, over 500 million tons of iron, 1 million tons of zinc, 600,000 tons of copper. One author calculated that the upper mile of crust could satisfy current consumption rates for copper for 500 million years. Much the same sort of calculation can be made for sea water. I am not suggesting that such dilute materials will ever be mined, but only indicating that exhaustion in a physical sense is meaningless. Of more immediate interest, some of the elements that are most important to society are available in the greatest quantity. Copper and zinc are relatively rare metals. Iron and aluminium are not: together with a few other elements, they make up much of the crust of the earth, and there are thousands of square miles that could be considered as low-grade iron and aluminium deposits, some of which will be mined in the future. The same can be said about phosphorus and potassium, the two critical mineral components for fertilizers.

Further, there is a strong tendency for many (perhaps most) mineral resources to increase in quantity as the quality that can be economically exploited goes down. This, too, is typically an exponential relationship, and in general terms it means there is much more

105

copper available at 0.5 per cent than at 0.6 per cent, more iron at 35 per cent than at 40 per cent, and so on. . . . Thus, the opportunity for technology to augment supplies is extensive. Indeed, where the new technology permitted an unconventional type of deposit to be mined, the increase could be very large. For example, the quantities of manganese, copper and nickel on the deep sea floor dwarf conventional sources, but recovering them is still too expensive. Even where only conventional sources are involved, the increase may be enough to still fears of exhaustion. Figures on the amount of copper available in just relatively concentrated deposits (those containing more than a 0.25 per cent copper, which even now is nearly within economic reach) permit us to calculate that there is a *two thousand year supply.*

Unfortunately, most descriptions of mineral resources include only the material that could be mined at today's prices and today's technology – what are properly termed 'reserves' – and thus quite understate their availability. The difference between reserves and resources becomes critically important when dealing with the so-called life index, the ratio of the reserves of some element to its current consumption. The resulting figure is best regarded as a sort of inventory of the stock on the shelf, so to speak, but it is sometimes mistakenly taken to mean the years remaining until exhaustion. . . . The real question, then, is not whether resources exist, but at what rate different sources of supply will become available to man in the sense of being *economically* feasible to recover. As stated most succinctly by the late American geographer, Erich W. Zimmermann, 'Resources are not; they become'. In other words, natural minerals do not become resources until they are combined with man's ingenuity. The record is impressive. Mineral resources have become more and more widely available despite (and partly because of) growing rates of consumption. Demand for minerals stimulates their supply. This, in crude form, is the modern economic view of mineral resources, or the 'cornucopian' view as it has been dubbed.

Consider the role of price. To an economist, a rising price for some commodity indicates increasing scarcity of supply relative to demand. This is what we should expect with minerals as depletion progresses. However, mineral prices have historically fallen in real terms as technology has more than overcome classical depletion. Supply has grown faster than demand.

True, in recent years price increases for minerals have been more common. However, we do not live in a world of pure competition, and we must not assume that recent price increases for many mineral commodities result from increasing long-run scarcity. . . .

I trust the reader will share my readiness to accept the foregoing assurances that neither this generation nor generations to come need have any serious misgivings as to the future in respect of continuity of supply of man's needs in the several types of mineral substances.

6. Multinational Inauguration of the System

F.1 INTERNATIONAL ADMINISTRATION IMPRACTICABLE. As was said in the preliminary sections of this book – following my quotation of Lord Bradbury's letter headed 'What is a £ Sterling?' as published in *The Times* – it would be wholly impracticable for the proposed system of conditional valorization of basic commodities to be inaugurated and administered internationally – for various reasons. The most potent of these is that there is no mutually-accepted international currency as there was – prior to August 1914 – when the Gold Standard was in effective operation. In the subsequent – ever-increasing – disorder in regard to currency exchange it would be quite impracticable to secure international agreement as to the levels in various countries (each with its own currency continuously altering in values domestically and externally) at which the *initial* Index should be set – in respect of even a single commodity. All manner of conflicting interests would be involved and interminable wrangling would be inevitable – and to no good purpose.

F.2 MULTINATIONAL ADOPTION FEASIBLE AND PROBABLE. (a) In contrast, unilateral adoption and administration of this system by any great commodity-*importing* nation is wholly feasible; and if HM Government in the United Kingdom (particularized as distinct from HM Governments in Canada, Australia and New Zealand) will set the example – in the sense that the Bank of England initiated the Gold Standard – there can be little if any doubt that other industrialized nations which depend on external sources for supplies of basic materials would, in their own interests, be quick to follow that example – for reasons not far to seek – see B.13.

(b) Why, it will doubtless be asked, should not any commodity-*exporting* country establish its own Price Stabilizing Authority? The answer is that, although it could do so if it so wished, it is doubtful that such action would achieve any useful result. Of course, if any one country has a monopoly of resources of an essential commodity which we may term 'Y', or if a group of the chief exporters of 'Y' can combine as the countries comprising the Organization of Petroleum Exporting Countries (OPEC) have done recently, such country (or group) can charge virtually what it likes for 'Y' – always provided that buyers are prepared to pay such price; at least unless and until other sources of supply of 'Y' become available. However, there is no analogy whatever to be drawn between the operations of such cartels as OPEC which (actuated by the profit motive if not also by political considerations) are able to restrict or increase supplies at will, and those of a PSC which has no profit or political actuation, nor any authority whatever in the matter of increasing or reducing supplies from external sources. In these respects producers are their own arbiters – with PSC providing a reliable 'indicator' which serves as a price-guide to exporters of every commodity within PSC's scope.

(c) Fortunately for highly industrialized nations, there are usually many sources from which the raw materials they need can be obtained; as basic producers in other lands for the most part eagerly compete for such importers' custom. Generally speaking, no advantage would accrue to any individual commodity-*exporting* nation's setting up its own PSC. Nevertheless, one illustration (among others that might be cited) of what *can* be done within a producing nation is provided by the operations of the Wool Commission in Australia which, when wool prices fall to an unduly low level, enters the market as a buyer; and, if and when it comes to hold stocks, it will sell if prices rise to remunerative levels. It is financed primarily by levies on commercial sales plus a measure of government subsidy. However, such operations are especially facilitated in respect of this particular product because foreign buyers flock to Australia to bid for their requirements at the auction marts in the several States. Moreover, that country is noted not only for the great volume of merino wool it produces but also for its high quality.

However, a situation could arise when the Commission's funds were in short supply and market offerings were in excess supply. And, in such circumstances, it could be very valuable if it were able to dispose of excessive holdings to (say) a British Price Stabilizing Corporation; because it would thus acquire sterling at the level of the relevant low *point* (which would be appropriately different for merino and crossbred types) with the knowledge that wool so bought could not be re-sold excepting at the relevant HIGH *point* – the level(s) of which all would be aware. Or, alternatively, that Commission could deposit its surplus – wholly or in part in PSC's custody against its *Warrants* – and then be in a strong position in regard to profferings on the British market (see B.15) as well as on adjacent Continental markets.

F.3 INTERNATIONAL INTER-DEPENDENCE.
(a) It has to be kept in mind that there are fundamental differences between the economic bases of highly industrialized nations (here termed Group 'I') and of preponderantly primary-producing countries (here termed Group 'P'). Of course, some nations qualify for inclusion in both these groups, with the USA and – though in lesser degrees – Canada and Australia as examples. However, there are very many countries which are more or less exclusively within one or other of these groups. The United Kingdom and Japan are noteworthy examples within the 'I' group; while – on the other hand – countries with Group 'P' include many whose peoples' well-being is dependent – largely if not wholly – upon the profitable export of maybe only one major product, e.g. Zambia upon copper, Ghana upon cocoa, Cuba and Mauritius – and others – upon cane-sugar. In short, what some countries need other countries are able to supply by exporting outputs in excess of their own domestic needs and using the money so derived for reciprocal purchases. The accumulation of commodity surpluses – financed internally – within any country which is itself a producer of that commodity serves no useful purpose and is certainly not economically viable (being of itself inflationary in the domestic sense) so long as there are alternative sources from which industrialized nations can obtain adequate supplies.

(b) The utopian ideal in the economic sense is a country which has the full range of its needs in primary and secondary form, and in essential services, within its own territory. As was shown in Chapter 5, that utopian ideal awaits realization within this world as a whole.

(c) However, in respect of one's assertion that any Price Stabilizing Corporation should be administered by a commodity-importing nation, it may suffice to say that the resulting advantages would be world-wide; whereas a PSC operated by a country whose economy is based for the most part – if not wholly – on receipts from exports of a limited range of basic materials would be merely internal in its effects, always subject to there being other countries able to export the same types of basics unless these or the great bulk of them were able to combine as in the case of OPEC.

F.4 MULTINATIONAL ADMINISTRATION.
(a) While it has always been my contention that no preliminary *Agreement* – in precise terms – would be required in advance of two or more industrialized nations' deciding to establish their own PSC's, following the example of the initiating nation, mere commonsense might be expected to be applied in such a manner as to achieve a desirable measure of concord – at least in principle. Thus, given that this system be initiated by the British Government with the administration of its PSC in line (in principle if not in detail) with the illustrative proposals in this work, it would be highly advantageous that (say) a German PSC should follow the general pattern as set by the initiating nation: (i) as to relating the *initial* Index of Commodity 'X' to its preceding annual average cost (cif) at German ports of entry; (ii) as to the percentages below and above Index at which low and HIGH *points* were set in Deutschmarks; (iii) as to the volume in a BLOCK being equivalent to one-tenth of preceding annual average tonnage imported; (iv) as to the extent to which Index and *points* would adjust automatically downwards in the event of BLOCK accumulation or upwards in the absence of intakes of reserves of 'X'; and (v) as to all its transactions in commodities subject to duty or excise (whether imposed by Germany or by the EEC) being under Customs and Excise Bond.

(b) Some such measure of *multi*national concord would seem likely to be mutually acceptable in that it would not in any way impinge upon the *status quo* of any nation unilaterally adopting this system. In the event, the advantages within the domestic economies of all such nations would (ultimately) equate – with this qualification: the magnetic influence (i.e., the 'drawing power' as expressed in attracting reserves) of any one nation's PSC would inevitably be the reciprocal purchasing power of the currency it disbursed in payment for its PSC's intakes. But no one could quarrel with that state of affairs which would depend upon the enterprise and industrial efficiency of the people in that country. In suggesting that the measure of concord indicated above might reasonably be anticipated, it is of great importance that all transactions under the proposed system's auspices should be under Customs and Excise Bond in cases where duties were levied in the normal way. This would give free access to the currency of each nation operating a PSC, in effect initiating – and maintaining – free trade in basic essential commodities, without any interference with the exaction of applicable duties on commodities passing out of its PSC's reserves into commercial usage.

(c) Thus would the dictum 'What is good for one is good for all' be given practical effect.

F.5 COMMODITIES TO FIND THEIR OWN PRICE LEVELS.
(a) In order to illustrate – in principle – this system in *multi*national operation suppose it came to be adopted by four highly industrialized nations with the United Kingdom, the USA, France and West Germany as examples. To relate the operation – or potential operation – of each of these four nations' Price Stabilizing Corporations (one to another) in respect of Commodity 'X', the following factors are hypothesized: (i) that the *initial* Index would be based upon the annual average of costs (cif) of 'X' during the immediately preceding quinquennium as in B.4 (relatively weighted – if then necessary – in respect of inflation and/or in consequence of increased freight charges); (ii) that the levels of the low and (conditional) HIGH *points* would be respectively 10 per cent below and above Index; (iii) that a BLOCK would be equivalent to

one-tenth of preceding annual average volume of 'X' imported; and (iv) that there would be an automatic reduction of (say) 5 per cent of the initial levels of Index-and-*points* values if the intakes by any PSC came to aggregate a first full BLOCK – with precisely the same reductions in such values (i.e. invariably by 5 per cent of *initial* levels) at the intake (if any) of a second BLOCK – and of any additional BLOCK of 'X' – with this process reversing automatically if any such holdings diminished (BLOCK by BLOCK).

(b) To facilitate comparisons – in the Table which follows – of values of individual nation's *initial* Index and *points* (one with the others) each set of national currencies is converted to sterling – at the exchange rates of: £1=US$2.4; French fr. 12; West German DM 8. And, further to facilitate the comparative effects of reductions (in each case of 5 per cent) in the event of a *first full* BLOCK being acquired, these too are converted to sterling. This procedure is adopted to bring to the surface the process by which – if and when there came to be BLOCK accumulations in all four of these nations – there would be a close harmonization in values of 'X' with fluctuations in its price being held within a price-band as established by the relevant low and (effective) HIGH *points*. And, of course, external exchange rates (in terms of 'X' – and of every other commodity of which reserves came to be held by any nation's PSC) would be correspondingly relatively stable.

Nations operating PSCs	Initial Index per ton	Initial low point per ton	Initial HIGH point per ton
UK	£100	£90	£110
of which 5%=	5.00	4.50	5.50
USA	$250	$225	$275
(Sterling value=	£104.16	£93.75	£114.58)
of which 5%=	5.20	4.68	5.72
France	Fr. 1,800	Fr. 1,062	Fr. 1,298
(Sterling value=	£98.33	£88.50	£108.16)
of which 5%=	4.91	4.42	5.40
W. Germany	D.M. 780	D.M. 702	D.M. 858
(Sterling value=	£97.50	£87.75	£107.25)
of which 5%=	4.87	4.88	5.36

113

(c) In this hypothetical Table the order of values per ton of the *initial* low *point* levels (second column) in comparable terms of sterling is: USA – £93.75; UK – £90.00; France – £88.50; and West Germany – £87.75. From this it would appear that, in the event of producers of 'X' failing to secure £93.75 (sterling equivalent of \$225) or better in commercial markets, they would sell to the US PSC. Keeping it in mind that what matters to the producer is his net receipts as at site of production, we here assume that the American low *point* is the most advantageous to him – in which event *its* PSC's acquisitions may sooner or later aggregate a first full BLOCK with its Index and *points* falling by 5 per cent (£4.68 in terms of sterling) to £89.07 in that currency. The UK low *point* at £90 would then be likely to attract reserves up to a first full BLOCK, when *its* low *point* would fall by £4.50 to £85.50 and the then best would be the French low *point* at the equivalent of £88.50 – unless a full BLOCK likewise accumulated in France, causing a 5 per cent (equivalent to £4.42) reduction in France's low *point*; when the German PSC's low *point* (at the equivalent of £87.75) would be the best offering.

F.6 NICE UNIFORMITY NOT TO BE EXPECTED.
(a) It is not suggested that anything like such uniformity in *initial* Index levels would come about. Very many factors might intervene, of which one would be that it would be most unusual for producers to consign direct to any PSC, which would normally be asked to buy only if and when supplies of 'X' had already arrived in the USA and/or in Britain, France or Germany; and when there was a buyers' market developing within the country in which there had come to be profferings that (unless recourse was had to its PSC) would cause commercial prices to decline steeply.

(b) Obviously the very fact that a PSC stood ready to operate *within* any importing country would have an unprecedentedly steadying effect on markets concerned with every commodity within that nation's PSC's scope – not only within that country but everywhere else.

F.7 BENIGN EFFECTS ON CURRENCIES. Early in this work it was shown that the equalizing of bargaining powers as between sellers and buyers, engendered especially by a PSC's readiness to accept deposits of commodities in its custody while still in commercial ownership, would tend to keep commercial prices close to the relevant Index level – midway between low and (effective) HIGH *points*. If the commodity-trading relationships, as between one nation's PSC or several national PSC's (on the one hand) and the very many commodity-*exporting* countries (on the other) be thought through, it will become evident that a corresponding degree of near parity of commodity-values would – in due course – come to obtain on not only a *multi*national but also on an *international* scale. And that would mean corresponding measures of parity as between different nations' currencies – in terms of the widest practicable range of the essential needs of men.

F.8   A POSSIBLE EEC STABILIZING CORPORATION.   As was mentioned in Chapter 1 (A.16) whether or not the United Kingdom is to remain a member of the EEC has not yet been finally decided. Whatever be the outcome of the proposed referendum, it would not be practical in the absence of a common currency for the Community (as such) to establish an Organization to function along the lines proposed for any *individual* great commodity importing-nation. Nevertheless, as described in F.4 above, it would be as practicable as it was desirable for each of several of the EEC Partners to come to a general agreement in regard to the details specified in F.4 – without any infringement of individual sovereignty. And such action could sooner or later assist towards a realization of the ideal of a common currency throughout the EEC; that is if and when each such stabilizing corporation came to hold substantial reserves as currency backing.

The boon that would accrue to basic producers overseas by their having assured floors at known price levels in all EEC markets would be inestimable. But for full advantage so to accrue it would be essential that transactions of each nation's PSC should be (a) exclusively in its own currency and (b) under Customs and Excise Bond when applicable – vide Chapter 2 (B.9). Thus, the developing countries would have access to the currency of each such nation – without tariff or quota hindrances; and thus would each commodity importing-nation (in the fullness of time) come to acquire reserves of those essential basics upon which their industrial super-structures are built – with continuity of supply within known price bands.

F.9 THE EEC *vis-à-vis* WORLD FOOD SUPPLY. It is suggested that the interests of the 'developing' countries – and of the hundreds of millions of the undernourished in vast territories that have not yet reached the status of being termed 'developing' (because instead of developing they are retrogressing) – should be kept constantly in mind. Thus, it should be the implemented policy of the advanced nations to produce the maximum amount of their own domestic requirements in essential food stuffs, especially of grain. In this regard, immense acreages are now devoted to the production of beet sugar, whereas cane sugar can be produced in developing countries and delivered at a much lower cost than that of beet sugar – while still ensuring good standards of living for the cane-growers. One realizes that beet is a valuable factor in rotational farming but its place can be taken by other root crops for use as animal feeding-stuffs. In such circumstances the great grain exporting-countries, notably the USA, Canada and Australia, would have more of this vital food to offer to the poor sections of the world. As to how this would be paid for is another matter currently engaging the World Food Conference which is meeting in Rome while this book is being printed. One can only hope for the best as to the outcome of that Conference's deliberations, in which regard see page 146 of 'In Conclusion.'

F.10 DEFLATION WITHOUT TEARS! If one's descriptions of this system's functioning has been as clear to the reader as one hopes, it will have become evident that inflation would reduce automatically in inverse ratio to BLOCK accumulation(s) if any; that is in terms of each – and of every – commodity so taken into PSC reserve. But this would not be politically-contrived deflation (if that be possible which is questionable to say the least); rather would it be a pattern of cause and effect under self-regulating influences of mutual advantage to producer and consumer.

F.11 PSCS COULD NOT 'COMPETE'. It has been suggested – by people who had not come fully to understand the working of this system – that it might lead to competition between different nations' PSCs, but that idea is untenable. However, suppose that – with some such objective in mind – Nation 'A' waited until several other countries had set up their Stabilizing Corporations, each announcing its *initial points*, and that Nation 'A' then followed suit – but with *initial points* very much higher than the others, with a view to providing special inducements to consignors. For it to do anything of the sort would mean that it was inducing deliberately self-imposed domestic inflation; and that it had overlooked the fact that without ever establishing its own PSC, it would at any time attract consignments simply by offering higher prices than those obtainable elsewhere – always provided that the sellers were satisfied with the reciprocal purchasing power of Nation 'A''s currency. It would be absurd to suggest that the mere setting-up of its own PSC would vest Nation 'A' with any special 'drawing power' as a buyer.

F.12 OVERALL ADVANTAGES. Always bearing in mind that there is no visible limit to the world's potential resources in the prime needs of men (given that intelligent co-operation – as indicated in the preceding chapter – which nature demands if she is to yield a full measure of her bounty), it must surely be evident that the best (and it seems to me the only) way in which to stabilize economy on a world-wide scale is by the establishment of 'reservoirs' of essential basic materials – accessible to all on as nearly as possible equivalent terms. Once again it is stressed that this must be a gradual process – especially in view of the leeway that has to be made good among that two-thirds of the world's people who are under-privileged and for a great part woefully undernourished. But, within a mere five years of this system's inauguration, much could be achieved; and by the end of a decade something approaching equitable economic good order in the international sense could have replaced that near-chaos which (according to the media) now appears to threaten.

F.13 A WORLD DISASTER RELIEF FUND. In Paragraph xiii of 'Author's Precis', when emphasizing that no Price Stabilizing Corporation would be actuated by the profit motive, I suggested that – if and when a British PSC's premiums had come to cover its administrative expenses (which would be negligible if the simple management procedures suggested in Chapter 3 were closely followed) – all additional money should be paid into a special Holding Account to form the nucleus of a Disaster Fund for the relief of distress in gravely afflicted regions in any part of the world. If a series of national PSC's would adopt precisely the same policy in this regard, a considerable aggregate amount of money might well accumulate. And, once substantial reserves had come to be established, even if there were no great monetary holdings, relief in many instances could be accorded by help in kind – particularly in basic foods such as grains. What is of transcending importance is that the functioning of the proposed system should be wholly divorced from profit-making; that its entire functioning should be characterized – and be *seen* to be actuated – by benevolence. It is my conviction that of men's attributes, benevolence is that which is most widely shared. And it is this innate human characteristic which calls for capitalization – at long last and to the full – cynics notwithstanding.

F.14 THE STRATEGIC ANGLE. Cynics (and not only cynics) will naturally ask 'What about the strategic implications involved?' 'What is to prevent any national Government's taking over its PSC's stocks (wholly or in part) to be strategically stockpiled?' The answer is that there would be nothing to prevent that happening – just as there is now nothing to prevent any nation (with the financial wherewithal) directly and/or obliquely entering world markets for the same purpose. And, in a similar sense – fragile agreements to the contrary – there is little to prevent further building up of nuclear armaments. But the fact that such devastating power is constantly 'at the disposal' of certain nations is of course its own great deterrent so far as the possible belligerents are concerned. It is not too far to stretch the analogy to point to the fact that the existence of large reserves of essential basics (for all of which realistic prices had been paid and which were accessible to all on like terms) would similarly be a deterrent in its own way in respect of international discords. It is surely true to say that, apart from racial and religious frictions, such discords are for the great part attributable to maladjusted economy. And this is true not only in the international sense but likewise within domestic spheres.

F.15 Let it not be thought that anything in the foregoing implies criticism of legitimate profit-making which is the very keystone of all productive enterprise.

7. Commodity Agreements and Price Maintenance

Forenote: The reason considerable space is devoted to this subject is that in correspondence with the author from HM Treasury, great store has from time to time been set on the British Government's favouring international commodity agreements to the unilateral inauguration of a British Price Stabilizing Corporation having the widest practicable range of products within its scope; and because, in the face of pressures from both sides of the House of Commons that the proposed system be at least fully investigated, answers from the Government Front Bench have usually likewise expressed preference for such agreements. Unfortunately – with the exception of the Commonwealth Sugar Agreement up until 1973 and the International Tin Agreement, which was successful over a considerable period – all have failed in achieving their objectives. That each would have had a much better chance of being successful if there had been a British PSC in the background must surely be clear to the reader who takes the trouble to comprehend this chapter.

G.1 MOTIVATIONS OF AGREEMENTS.

(a) The actuating motives behind international commodity agreements are economically and politically admirable. All are designed to lead to fair deals as between basic producers themselves, on the one hand, and user-buyers on the other, which objectives are in close accord with those of a Price Stabilizing Corporation. For example, take those of the International Tin Agreement, which are:

(i) To prevent or alleviate widespread unemployment or underemployment and other serious difficulties which are likely to result from maladjustments between supply and demand for tin;

(ii) to prevent excessive fluctuation in the price of tin and to achieve a reasonable degree of stability of price on a basis which will secure long-term equilibrium between supply and demand;

(iii) to ensure adequate supplies of tin at reasonable prices at all times; and

(iv) to provide a framework for the consideration and development of measures to promote the progressively more economic production of tin while protecting tin deposits from unnecessary waste or premature abandonment.

(b) However, the means whereby the attainment of such objectives is sought differ markedly from those which a PSC would adopt – if in conformity in principle with what has been outlined in this book. The Tin Agreement will be described in some detail later. Suffice it to say here that its functioning (which is most closely related to that of the proposed system) achieved a considerable measure of success over protracted periods of years. But it encountered many difficulties that would not have been likely to arise if there had been in the background a PSC standing ready to operate in respect of tin.

G.2 SUPERFICIALLY CONFLICTING INTERESTS. The problem facing those concerned with the negotiations of commodity agreements are manifold. In the first place there is always a seeming conflict of interests between 'producer parties' and 'consumer parties' – something which obscures the real facts, which are that the interests of both these sets of 'parties' are complementary. The superficial conflict between them is that, while the producer seeks to obtain as high a price as possible, the consumer seeks to pay as low a price as possible. In this regard more than one journal has commented, in comparing the system I advocate with the results of commodity agreements, in such terms as those which appeared in *The Director* (February 1958):

In the past, piecemeal schemes for 'orderly marketing' [i.e. under commodity agreements] of basic materials almost always led to restriction of supply. When prices were stabilized, they finished up too high.

And in the same context, *The Guardian* had this to say:

121

Most schemes for commodity price stability rely too much on altruism, and call for international co-operation that is not forthcoming.

G.3 ABSENCE OF RESERVES EMASCULATING. Unless the organization administering any commodity agreement has the authority – and financial resources – constantly to stand ready to buy the relevant product at a pre-notified price, there can be no assured floor in the market; and, unless the same organization comes to acquire reserves in the shape of supplies that cannot find buyers at not less than its own purchasing price, it cannot establish a market ceiling. Moreover, if the 'producer parties' to an agreement have themselves to provide (or partially to provide) the essential funds (as for the Tin Buffer Stock scheme) they are being merely prudent if they trim their outputs so as to avoid the necessity for 'buying their own wares' – something the writers of the excerpts from *The Director* and *The Guardian* doubtless had in mind.

No single commodity agreement operating in isolation in respect of a single product can *per se* achieve other than partial success; because it is not so much the actual price received by the producer and that paid by the user-buyer that most matters. Rather is it the relativity of the value of one commodity in terms of other products. That is why it is essential that the widest practicable range of durable basics should be brought within a Price Stabilizing Corporation's range.

G.4 FRUSTRATING FACTORS.
(a) The following are among the difficulties confronting the negotiators concerned:

(i) Unless an agreement embraces all significant national groups of producer-exporters, and all significant relevant importing-nations, those not committed to that agreement are its potential saboteurs.

(ii) Although 'exporting parties' on the one hand agree to supply prescribed quotas to 'importing parties', and the latter agree to purchase such quotas from the 'exporting parties' – there are no effective sanctions possible (nor would they be desirable) in the case of non-fulfilment on either side.

(iii) Excepting that of the International Tin Council, no international agreement (up until late 1972) provided for the establishment of reserves that, under the ITC, are termed 'buffer stocks', the means of acquiring which are described in G.10 *et seq.*

(b) It needs to be mentioned here that the necessary funds from which to pay for such stocks had to be provided – under the first post-war Agreement by the tin-producers themselves, although – under subsequent Agreements – user-buyers like-wise contributed (at least in respect of administrative costs). In the event, from time to time over the years, the ITC ran short of funds; and, in 1973, the whole thing got out of hand.

G.5 INTERNATIONAL WHEAT AGREEMENTS.
(a) If what now follows savours of the historical it is because the onset of the inflation which now plagues the free world was demonstrably largely due to the strange activities of the US Commodity Credit Corporation – already referred to in Chapter 5. Under the first post-war International Wheat Agreement (of 1940–53) the United States, Canada, Australia and France jointly agreed to supply 41 importing countries with 12 million tons of wheat annually during the four years covered by that Agreement. Each importing nation undertook to buy a prescribed minimum with the UK taking $4\frac{1}{2}$ million tons. The agreed minimum price for 1949–50 (crop year ending 31 July) was to be US 150 cents but it was to fall in 1950–51 to 140 cents, in 1951–52 to 130 cents, and in 1952–53 to 120 cents. The maximum price, however, was to remain constant at 180 cents over the whole period. These prices related to a high-grade Canadian wheat (No. I Manitoba) as at Fort William/Port Arthur on the shores of the Great Lakes flanking the US and Canadian borders. For other grades prices were to be negotiated between the maximum and minimum as prescribed.

(b) At the time this Agreement was signed the exporting countries were holding a carry-over from preceding seasons of nearly 12 million tons, and it therefore seemed reasonable to expect that – if the average output was at least maintained in succeeding years and demand did not substantially increase – prices would fall more or less in proportion to the declining scale permitted under the IWA, the declared purpose of which was to 'ensure supplies of wheat to importing countries at equitable and stable prices'.

(c) It is evident that it must then have been considered by the exporting parties to that Agreement than an annual decline in minimum price by 10 cents per bushel from 150 down to as low as 120 cents would be equitable – provided output continued at least at normal levels. In the event, however, notwithstanding that there was an unprecedented series of bountiful seasons – with yields per acre far above average – the IWA wheat price was *maintained* throughout those four years at the *maximum* of 180 cents. Demand did not increase, and, in that period, surpluses (in the four exporting countries) rose to exceed 25 million tons, sufficient to provide the importing countries with over two years' supply without the production of one more bushel.

(d) The reason for this strange state of affairs was not far to seek. The US Commodity Credit Corporation is the instrument whereby a system of progressively rising price-support for wheat (and for other farm products) is implemented within America. And, notwithstanding that the USA – as a party to the IWA – had undertaken to provide 5 million tons *at a maximum of* 180 cents a bushel, its Government-financed CCC guaranteed to American growers *a minimum price in* 1949–50 *of* 199 *cents*; *in* 1950–51 *of* 218 *cents; in* 1951–52 *of* 220 *cents; and in* 1952–53 *of* 221 *cents*! Thus throughout those four years the CCC's guaranteed price was at least 19 cents, and up to 41 cents, higher than the IWA's ceiling price of 180 cents. But that is only part of the story, because though many more millions of tons of wheat passed into CCC's surplus, the prices in the free (?) American domestic market were always much higher than the CCC's 'support' price; and, in order to provide its quota under the IWA, the American Government had to pay to growers a price that included the difference between the internal *market* price on day of purchase and that obtained under the International Wheat Agreement. In 1953 the Director of Finance of the Department of Agriculture testified that the American Government had to provide $174 million for the privilege of supplying that nation's quota under the International Wheat Agreement. The situation was even more unsatisfactory in succeeding years. That such a state of affairs was astonishingly anomalous is beside the point – it is what occurred.

While it would not seem necessary further to elaborate upon the antics of the CCC, a modicum of light relief may not be here out of context.

G.6 'GOING INTO THE NOT-RAISING-HOGS BUSINESS'. The CCC's progressively rising price-support policy led to such vast surpluses of so many farm products, ranging from raw cotton to a 'butter mountain' (with *market* prices rising to extortionate heights) that the CCC had recourse to (then*) hardly credible tactics. In that connection, Senator Barry Goldwater (Republican, Arizona) had inserted in Congressional Records (in February 1958) the following letter from one of his constituents:

Dear Mr Senator,

My friend Bordeaux, over in Pima county, received a $1,000 check from the Government this year for not raising 50 hogs. So I am going into the not-raising-hogs business myself next year.

What I want to know is, in your opinion, what is the best kind of hog not to raise? The hardest work in this business is going to be to keep an inventory of how many hogs I have not raised. I plan to operate on a small scale at first, holding myself down to about 4,000 hogs, which means I will have $80,000. Now these hogs I will not raise will not eat 100,000 bushels of corn.

I understand that you also pay farmers for not raising corn. So will you pay me anything for not raising 100,000 bushels of corn not to feed the hogs I am not raising?

P.S. Can I raise ten or twelve hogs on the side – just enough to get a few sides of bacon to eat?

It was indeed an astonishing state of affairs. With one hand the CCC was disbursing large sums among farmers NOT to produce this, that or the other commodity; and, with the other, it was pouring out hundreds of millions of dollars in payment for all manner of products to be held as sterile hoards – setting at nought the basic law of supply and demand. Thus was domestic inflation actually fostered – and by a Government agency; and *it quickly extended outwards*.

*The word 'then' is interpolated because in recent years we have seen a similar policy put into effect within the European Economic Community under the Common Agricultural Policy.

THE EEC COMMON AGRICULTURAL POLICY.

No doubt the reader will have it in mind that certain aspects of the EEC CAP are unhappily closely in line with those put into effect by the US CCC with most unfortunate consequences. In this regard it may suffice to point to the fact that up until 1970 half a million cows were slaughtered in France in order to reduce output of milk products – the farmers being liberally paid for such destruction out of EEC funds. And this in a world in which perhaps two-thirds of the people are undernourished and millions literally starving – verily a case of, 'I'm all right Jack! *Ou peut-être chacun pour soi!*'.

Fortunately, the CAP is currently under review largely due to pressures from the British Government.

G.7 EXTERNAL REPERCUSSIONS.

(a) Reverting to the IWA, the effect in neighbouring Canada on wheat prices – both internal and external – was inevitable. The US quota represented over 40 per cent of total IWA exports, and the Americans would not further subsidize that quota to enable their wheat to be sold at less than the 180 cents maximum. In such circumstances it was not to be expected that Canada would offer her share (generally of higher grade than American wheat) at lower than that figure; and Australia and France fell into line. So it was that the cost to the consumers in the 41 importing nations (that were parties to the IWA) continued to be maintained at artificially high level – while the CCC went on holding huge stocks until the sequence of events set down in Chapter 5 (E.14(e)) (treating of US disposals to Communist countries). Once again it is stressed that grains are not only the most important of men's foods the world over; they are also highly important as feeding-stuffs for livestocks – especially for the production of meats and of dairy-and-poultry products. If the manifest intention of the International Wheat Agreement of 1949–53 (and of subsequent IW Agreements) had not been frustrated by the CCC, prices of grains would have fallen from year to year – and living costs (to the extent that these depend on food prices) would have reduced by gradual process through the forty-one countries that were the importing parties to the IW Agreement; and indeed throughout the free world.

(b) What a different story it would have been if the International Wheat Council had been adequately provided with funds that would have enabled it to have established wheat reserves – as under the Tin Buffer Stock scheme – and if the Commodity Credit Corporation had operated a system in line with that proposed for a Price Stabilizing Corporation.

G.8 THE INTERNATIONAL WHEAT COUNCIL'S SITUATION IN MID-1974. In late 1974 the whole wheat situation is in a state of flux with the International Wheat Council powerless. All that can be said of it is that it is 'keeping the general wheat situation under constant review'. But, if and when its necessarily revised provisions are put into effect, it will need to have some provision for the establishment of buffer stocks if its long-term policy is to be effective. And, of course, with any great wheat-importing nations having in operation a Price Stabilizing Corporation, the establishment of buffer stocks by the IWC would be greatly facilitated.

G.9 OTHER INTERNATIONAL FOOD-STUFFS AGREEMENTS. There are three other food products in respect of which there are International Agreements involving producing- and consuming-countries, each of which should perhaps be here dealt with shortly. But in the event – as with wheat – all are currently in a state of flux.

(a) SUGAR.

Commonwealth Agreement. There are two agreements in respect of this product, one the Commonwealth Sugar Agreement and the other the International Sugar Agreement. Of these the CSA functioned with considerable success from 1951 onwards until disrupted by Britain's overtures and eventual entry to the EEC. However, no corresponding measure of success has ever been achieved under the International Sugar Agreement. The CSA was between the United Kingdom, as a single importing party, and the several cane-sugar producing countries within the Commonwealth which jointly undertook to provide (and Britain undertook to buy) an aggregate of 1,717,000 tons annually – with the following quotas allotted to the exporting Members:

West Indies	725,000	Fiji	140,000	British Honduras	20,000
Mauritius	380,000	Swaziland	85,000	East Africa	7,000
Australia	335,000	India	25,000		

(Prior to November 1965 Rhodesia was a party to the CSA with a quota of 25,000 tons.)

The agreed price cif British port in 1965 was £42 a ton, but this was subsequently adjusted upwards to £50 for the period 1972 to 1974. Excepting Australia, those listed are 'developing' countries and, as such, they were all paid a slightly higher rate (some £6 a ton) than that received by Australian growers. For the most part the exporting countries were able consistently to meet their quotas but if any one country was unable so to do the shortfall could be re-allocated to other exporting Members. Outputs, if any, in excess of the overall quota figure were saleable on what was termed the 'free market', which is that with which the International Sugar Agreement is concerned. As has been said, all went well with the CSA until 1968 when it became apparent that the British Government, if it entered the EEC, might not be able to continue its contractual obligations under the CSA.

In June 1971 Britain had proposed to the Six that the Community should continue to take the 'negotiated price sugar' of the *developing* countries and that the Australian quota should be '*phased out*' *over a period*. The Six did not agree to this, but undertook to 'have at heart' the interests of developing countries, particularly those which depended on sugar. HM Government and Governments of developing countries interpreted this assurance to mean 'a secure and continuing market in the enlarged Community on fair terms for the quantities of sugar, covered by the CSA, in respect of all its existing developing Member countries'. This interpretation was twice conveyed to Brussels (in 1971 and 1973) but it evoked no comment from the Council of Ministers.

No good purpose would be served by attempting here to elaborate further what has since transpired (or not transpired), particularly as the situation alters from month to month – if not from day to day – pending the outcome of the present British Government's efforts to effect amendments of the conditions (especially in respect of the Community Agricultural Policy) which obtained at date of UK's joining the EEC – January 1973.

The position at time of writing is that the current CSA expires at the end of 1974. The EEC has reached no decision on its future sugar policy with regard to the Commonwealth, and it has not even any definite propositions before it. The Commonwealth Sugar Exporters are therefore completely without security, except for the somewhat vague assurance that the EEC 'has at heart' the interests of developing countries.

N.B. Subsequent to my writing the above, when sugar was in grievously short supply within Britain the Minister for Agriculture, Mr T. F. Peart, was widely applauded that (in mid-October 1974) he was able to obtain from the EEC sources 150,000 tons at a cost of £150 per ton – the theory being that the EEC would purchase at world free-sugar prices (then around £400 a ton) and make up the difference out of EEC (presumably CAP) funds. For some weeks previously Mr Peart had been in negotiations with Australian sugar exporters (who were to be excluded or 'phased out' under the CSA negotiated price arrangements as above). Such 'phasing out' had led to the Australian growers making other – and much more profitable – arrangements for the sale elsewhere of their sugar. Let it suffice to say here that if they had not been excluded from the (still vague) 'advantages' which were to remain with the developing parties to the CSA, *they would have continued to supply the UK with their negotiated quota of 380,000 tons annually at least up until the end of 1974.* That certain Caribbean countries failed fully to meet *their* quotas at the negotiated price – deciding instead to sell at some six times that price on the free market – is beside the point. There would have been no possibility that the Australians would have failed to honour their commitments. The excuse for the action of those countries which failed fully to fulfil their commitments at the negotiated price, if somewhat reprehensible, is at least understandable in view of the fall in the reciprocal buying power – due to inflation – of what they received under the the CSA negotiated price.

Lest anyone should believe that the sugar deal with the EEC betoken that the UK was benefiting from that Community's largesse, it may be mentioned that on 25 October,

E

it was announced in Brussels that Britain's proportionate contribution (from date of entry) would be well in excess of the EEC's gross domestic product (*The Times*, 26 October, 1974).

International Agreement. Following earlier International Sugar Agreements in 1953 and 1958 – which development in the world market had rendered obsolete – in 1968 at a Conference of the United Nations Conference for Trade and Development (UNCTAD) a new Agreement was negotiated to extend to the end of 1973. Its objectives were similar to those of the International Tin Council (G.1) with special provisions: (a) for the protection of the developing countries; and (b) for the encouragement of sugar consumption, particularly in countries where 'consumption per capita is low'. Clearly at this time it was felt that additional demand could be met.

Under this (and indeed the previous) Agreements, the price stabilization aimed at was essentially based on a system of export quotas, the regulation of which was designed to bring total supplies available to the free market into balance with the requirements of that market. In effect this tended to restrict output in order to prevent over-supplying resulting in market collapse (as in 1967). To this end, the Agreements established basic export tonnages for each exporting country which were to serve as the basis for the allocation and adjustment of export quotas during each quota (calendar) year. Whilst no limitation was placed on any upward adjustment of total or individual quotas, the Agreements provided that quotas of individual countries could not be reduced below a certain percentage (under the 1968 Agreement 90 per cent, and in exceptional cases 85 per cent, of their respective basic export tonnages).

In effect, if growers produced to full capacity and there were favourable seasons prices probably would have again fallen far below actual production costs because the ISA had no system whereby surpluses to market absorption at or above prenotified levels could have been taken into reserve. Under PSC auspices a very different order of affairs would have obtained.

(b) COCOA.

The most recent international commodity agreement to be conceived is the International Cocoa Agreement 1972, which came into operation in the following year. Its objectives conformed in principle to those of the International Tin Council (G.1) and, as with all commodity agreements, it was born of good intention.

Like the ITA it provides for the establishment of a buffer-stock – up to a maximum of 250,000 tons – which the Buffer-Stock Manager would be responsible for administering, to maintain the 'floor' and 'ceiling' prices of cocoa at 23 cents per pound and 32 cents per pound respectively as in New York. The role of the Buffer Stock Manager being analogous to his counterpart in the ITA whose functions are described in G.10. It does however differ from the ITA as to its method of the financing of the buffer-stock. The Cocoa Agreement provides for a levy to be charged either 'on first export' or 'first import' of not more than one US cent per pound, with provision for this levy to be reduced depending on the 'financial resources of the Organization in relation to the buffer-stock'. Contributions from member countries have indeed come in regularly and in late 1974 had passed the US $20 million mark. But, as yet, there have not been any cocoa reserves acquired to form a buffer stock of this product.

With only a short existence to date, comment on the effectiveness of this Agreement would be out of place at this juncture. But it would clearly facilitate the chances of its being a success if a PSC stood in the background, most certainly not seeking to 'steal the scene' but providing an effective backcloth.

(c) COFFEE.

A runaway upsurge of demand for coffee in the immediate post-war years produced a (till then) unparalleled boon for growers with the price in New York reaching 93 cents in March 1954 – with world-wide effects. This prompted a flood of new plantings with the result that by the late 1950s production had so exceeded consumption that, in October 1962, the NY price fell to a mere 33 cents – again with world-wide effects. The coffee-producing countries sensing the danger of continuing market collapse began to explore the possibilities of international co-operation, and in 1962 the first International

Agreement was signed. Its objectives were similar to those of the International Sugar Agreement as was its price stabilizing mechanism, i.e., functioning by means of maximum export quotas – thereby to restrict potential outputs – for each producing country in an endeavour to sustain a minimum price level. To that end, during the period of that Agreement, from the seasons 1963–64 to 1967–68 *approximately one-third of the coffee trees planted in Brazil (a major-producer) were up-rooted!*

The second Agreement (1968) continued the export quota of the first Agreement and also set out to tackle what was regarded as the problem of over-production. Each country was required to present an acceptable National Coffee Policy Plan which would lead to the production of sufficient *but not excessive* quantities. In the event, severe frosts greatly affected much of the crop in 1969 and 1972 in the State of Parana (Brazil), and consequently there were serious falls in outputs in 1970 and 1973. By 1972–73 the world supply and demand for this product were approximately in balance and quite small seasonal changes in supply had marked effects on prices.

The 1968 Agreement, like that of 1962, contributed significantly to the stabilization of prices *but it was not designed to cope with extended periods of 'tight supplies' (essential to consumer interest) which developed late in 1972*; and which placed severe upward pressures on prices. It proved impossible to reconcile producer and importer interests as necessary to continue the operation of the 1968 Agreements quota adjustment provisions, and thus the economic provisions of the Agreement were allowed to lapse for the final nine months of the 1968 Agreement (January–September 1973) and coffee entered a period of relatively free trade. As at date of writing it would appear that there is no International Coffee Agreement in operation though the International Coffee Organization is being retained for negotiation of a possible third Agreement and as a competent authority for the collection and dissemination of coffee statistics and other information on world production, trade and consumption. Manifestly with a PSC in the background with coffee producers guaranteed known minimum prices the negotiation of a further Agreement would be greatly facilitated.

G.10 INTERNATIONAL TIN AGREEMENT.

(a) This Agreement is dealt with at some length because its objectives (which it successfully achieved over various periods of years) have been closely in line with those of a Price Stabilizing Corporation. In this regard – back in the mid-thirties – I had several discussions with the late Oliver Lyttelton (afterwards Viscount Chandos) who was one of the architects of the first International Tin Agreement.

Although the general reader may not be interested in the detailed operation of the ITC's efforts to maintain a constant tin 'price-band', it is here necessary at least to summarize what can only be characterized as the complexities and uncertainties that hamper such functioning. Those who trouble to read what immediately follows will, no doubt, contrast the intricacies as set down with the simplicity of a PSC's functioning.

Between 1930 and 1937 there were three Agreements – with objectives as listed in G.1 – all designed to counteract severe oscillations in prices. The third of these, to which seven countries (all producing) subscribed, was that of 1937–41 under which it was decided to establish a buffer stock of some 15,000 tons, in an effort to keep prices between £200 and £230 per ton – a cash margin of £30 equivalent to 15 per cent of the minimum. And that sized buffer stock had been established wholly by producing-countries by July 1939. But the scheme was thrown out of gear by the war – which led to that Agreement being wound up.

In March 1954, a new Agreement came into potential effect but it differed markedly as to its constituent Members from its predecessors, in that those subscribing to it included Governments of both tin-*producing* countries and tin-*importing* nations. This Agreement (at time of writing in its fourth term, but coming up for review in 1975) has been continually updated both in respect of its text and as to the nature of buffer stock operations. Currently, twenty-nine countries are parties to it of which seven are *producing*- and twenty-two *consuming*-nations. That all these countries are of one mind in desiring stability in tin costs is an earnest of the general wish for realistic stabilization of prices over the widest possible range of essential commodities.

(b) The administration of the ITC's policies is entrusted to a

Buffer Stock Manager. His activities are specifically governed by Article 25 from which the following are excerpts – with this qualification, that the italicized phrasings are not so printed in that article.

(1) The Manager shall be responsible for the operation of the buffer stock and in particular for buying, selling and maintaining stocks of tin in accordance with the provisions of this Article and of Article XI.

(2) If the price of cash tin on the London Metal Exchange –
   (a) is equal to or greater than the ceiling price, the Manager shall, *if he has tin at his disposal* –
      (i) offer tin for sale on the London Metal Exchange at the ceiling price, until either the cash price on the London Metal Exchange falls below the ceiling price *or the tin at his disposal is exhausted*;
      (ii) accept bids for tin at the ceiling price, adjusted for location and such other factors as may be determined by the Chairman, direct from consumers in participating countries or agents acting directly on their behalf, provided that the minimum tonnage of all such transactions shall be 5 tons and larger tonnages shall be in multiples of 5 tons; provided also that the Manager in accepting such direct bids shall have regard to the fair and equitable disposal of tin in the buffer stock;
   (b) *is in the upper third* of the range between the floor and ceiling prices, the Manager may offer tin for sale on the London Metal Exchange at the market price *if he considers it necessary* to prevent the market price from rising too steeply;
   (c) *is in the middle third* of the range between the floor and ceiling prices, the Manager shall neither buy nor sell unless the Council by a distributed simple majority decides otherwise;
   (d) *is in the lower third* of the range between the floor and ceiling prices, the Manager may buy cash tin on the London Metal Exchange at the *market* price if he considers it necessary to prevent the market price from falling too steeply;
   (e) *is equal to or less than the floor price*, the Manager shall, *if he has funds at his disposal*, offer to buy cash tin

on the London Metal Exchange at the floor price until either the cash price on the London Metal Exchange is above the floor price or *the funds at his disposal are exhausted.*

(3) At any time when under the provision of paragraph 2 of this Article the Manager may buy or sell cash tin on the London Metal Exchange, he may, within the framework of the general instruction he may have received,

(a) buy or sell three-months tin on the London Metal Exchange;

(b) buy or sell either cash or *forward* tin on any other established market for tin.

(4) Notwithstanding the provisions of this article the Council may authorize the Manager, *if his funds are inadequate to meet his operational expenses,* to sell sufficient quantities of tin at the current market price to meet his current operational expenditure.

In July 1972 because of the floating of the pound the situation was somewhat further complicated by a change of venue for Buffer Stock Quotations from London to Penang with 'floor' and 'ceiling' prices expressed in Malayan dollars per picul. At time of writing these stand respectively at 850 and 1,050 Malayan dollars per picul. But the principles governing this scheme's operations have in no wise changed.

CONTRASTING SIMPLICITY OF PSC'S FUNCTIONING.

(a) The fundamental difference between the foregoing and the proposed simple functioning of a Price Stabilizing Corporation is that the International Tin Council seeks to ensure both floor and ceiling prices, to achieve which:

(i) it needs to have funds available to absorb all tin offering at below the floor prices; and

(ii) it must have tin stocks to meet all demands made upon it for the supply of tin at the ceiling price.

In contrast PSC would guarantee only a floor price; but, subject to *predictable minor* adjustment, it would provide an absolutely firm assurance in that regard. Whether or not the PSC could provide a ceiling would be conditional upon its having acquired reserves at its low *point.* But, if and when PSC ceiling became effective, market price movements (on the suggested gearing) would be limited to 22.2 per cent. It is not without significance that after attempting to establish price bands of up to $37\frac{1}{2}$ per cent, the ITC in 1972 adopted one of 22.2 per cent, which has been advocated by the author over many decades. So far as the Tin Council is concerned, in order to be able to function successfully it would need to be in as relatively strong a position financially (in relation to its possible commitments as a tin buyer) and in respect of its tin holdings (in relation to its possible commitments as a seller of tin) as was the Bank of England when it was maintaining both a floor price and a ceiling price for gold!

The outstanding difference between the foregoing and the proposed simple functioning of a Price Stabilizing Corporation hardly needs elaboration but two points require emphasis: (i) whereas the Buffer Stock Manager's tin holdings at any given time are known only to himself, stocks, if any, held by PSC are constantly publicized; and (ii) the operations of the Buffer Stock Manager would be greatly facilitated if he could have recourse to PSC as and when necessary.

8. Questions and Author's Replies

The following are among the points raised by people to whom the foregoing chapters were shown in typescript; and, as the same sort of questions may arise in the minds of readers of the printed text, each is set down with the author's replies.

H.1 INITIAL INDEX LEVEL. Why is it suggested that the *initial* Index should be based upon the quinquennial average of costs at British ports of entry?

Reply: A five-year period of average costs is taken as the basis for the *initial* Index because, on the one hand, the activities and costings of producer-exporters to the UK (and to other countries) would have been more or less geared to such average; and in some instances virtually the whole economy of an exporting country (e.g., Mauritius – in respect of sugar) may have been so geared; and on the other hand, the activities of the user-industrialists concerned – and *their* costings – would likewise have become adapted to such averages. The cost at British port of entry is taken as a basis for the *initial* Index because that figure is constant in its incidence – that is in respect of the factors that it embraces.

H.2 LOCATION OF RESERVES. Why is no provision suggested for PSC to stand ready to buy and establish reserves in a country of origin?

Reply: There are four major reasons:
   (i) This would involve the acquisition of the currency of that country (at indeterminate rates of exchange), whereas all PSC's transactions are in sterling;
   (ii) the administrative difficulties and expenses involved would be immeasurable; and ultimate physical control

of such reserves (in the event of strained relations – as
with Uganda) would rest with the country in which
they were held;

(iii) it is the innate objective of this system that if and when
reserves were held they should be readily and immediately accessible to user-industrialists *within* the United
Kingdom; and

(iv) because international discords might seriously hamper
shipping – even though the UK was not directly
involved in such discords.

H.3 DOMESTICALLY PRODUCED BASICS. Why is it suggested
that PSC should not be concerned with domestically produced
commodities?

Reply: At least in so far as agricultural and pastoral products
are concerned, this question is answered in Chapter 2 (B.25).
As to metals, there would be no reason why these should not
be eligible for inclusion within PSC's scope – though it would
seem highly unlikely that domestically mined metals would be
proffered. However, in regard to coal, this seems to be the
place in which to strike another somewhat historical note.

When in the mid-thirties I was District Commissioner for
the Special (Depressed) Areas in West Cumberland, I made
representations to the then Chief Commissioner for all the
Special Areas in England and Wales – the late Sir P. Malcolm
Stewart – that the idle and semi-idle coal mines in Cumberland,
Durham-and-Tyneside and South Wales, should be got into
full production on the following – or some similar – basis:

That there should be established a Government-financed
Coal Reserves Corporation under which mine-owners
would be guaranteed prices (for each of the chief grades of
coal) which in the average would cover only actual production costs (then around fifteen shillings a ton – if my
memory serves me aright) for all coal delivered to that
Corporation's dumps – reasonably adjacent to their collieries;
and subject to an undertaking by this Corporation that
*none of the coal so purchased by it would be sold commercially
excepting at a mutually agreed premium* (and 15 to 20 per
cent was suggested as a basis for discussion). Moreover, it
was to be a condition that only unemployed miners

(registered as such) should be engaged – with no other additional men being so employed excepting with the specific approval of the CR Corporation.

Under such an arrangement, the mine-owners would have sold the usual amount of coal commercially, with the market price free to rise to that at which the CR Corporation (if and when it had come to hold stocks) would sell on demand to collecting buyers – and only in pre-specified large tonnages. It would have been from their commercial sales that mine-owners would have got their profits – and the greater the output from any mining-unit the cheaper the production costs (relative to overheads and servicing of capital). Sites were tentatively selected for dumps chiefly in valleys that were already served by old railway-lines – and deposits in these were to be turfed over to preserve calorific values. All other relevant plans were worked out after consultations with mine owners and with an eminent firm of Civil Engineers (Alexander Gibb & Partners). The idea was that – as there then appeared to be a considerable surplus of skilled miners available – the natural decrease in such numbers should be off-set by the establishment of readily accessible reserves, instead of such coal having to be prised from its parent deposits – often miles out under the Irish Sea. But it would be up to the CR Corporation to exercise prudence in authorizing employment of 'new' miners as and when deemed necessary.

Sir Malcolm Stewart strongly favoured this proposal and endorsed it to the then Minister of Labour (Mr Ernest Brown); but it was not accepted by the Government. If that recommendation had been put into effect from 1935 onwards, in all the Special Areas, it would have resulted in tens of millions of tons being held in easily accessible reserve when war broke out in September 1939. Moreover, such action would have gone a long way towards solving the then problem of unemployment, not only in mining but upwards throughout the economic superstructure. Instead, the nation continued to maintain hundreds of thousands of potential producers in demoralizing idleness at levels of mere subsistence. So it was that when war broke out coal had to be imported from America at a cost of over £4 a ton – with irreparable loss of many seamen and their ships.

I trust I may be forgiven for further reminiscing in this context. In August 1959 – when the coal industry was being run down in favour of oil usage – I submitted a long Memorandum to the Coal Board the opening paragraph of which read:

Coal is the only indigenous basic commodity in which the United Kingdom is self-sufficient. Yet our enjoyment of this fundamental advantage is being deliberately diminished – a process out of which economic, political, social and potentially grave strategic problems arise. It is suggested that coal production and usage in the UK should not be considered in isolation, but as one department of what might be termed a Quadrumvirate of inter-dependent nationalized enterprises of which the other three are the British Electric Authorities, the National Gas Boards, and British Railways.

I need not deal further with that Memorandum beyond suggesting that, if the proposals it contained had then been implemented, Britain would not have been in the parlous situation in respect of electric-power-generation which confronted us when the Organization of Petroleum Producers took the measures it adopted in late 1973.

H.4 ACCEPTABILITY OF STERLING. As the United Kingdom now has an increasing adverse visible balance running at the rate of some £3,000 to £4,000 million annually, is it likely that overseas primary producers would sell to the Corporation in exchange for payments in sterling?

Reply: If the overseas producer was not prepared to accept sterling, we should certainly be in a sorry plight, but in fact such external producers continue to supply us with some half our needs in food-stuffs and with over 80 per cent of our raw materials, and there is no valid reason why they should not increase their exports to this country. Of course, their readiness so to do would depend upon the reciprocal buying power of sterling so acquired, in which regard our manufacturers would be in a much better position to stabilize (if not to reduce) their selling prices if afforded continuity of supply of raw materials likewise at stable if not reduced costs.

H.5 OBSOLESCENCE? What would be the position of PSC if it found itself in possession of very large reserves of some product the use of which had greatly diminished (and which was continuing to diminish) owing to competition from synthetics or from alternative natural substances?

Reply: To qualify for valorization under PSC's auspices a commodity would need to be convertible into a wide range of consumer and/or capital goods that were in widespread and continuing demand. So it follows that no commodity would have been valorized if there had been a *likelihood* of its becoming obsolete to the extent contemplated in the question. From time to time in the past it was suggested that, for example, because of increasing outputs of synthetic rubber it might become unprofitable to produce plantation rubber. The best judges in this matter are the rubber-growing companies whose policy has not been to reduce their outputs but rather to reduce their production costs (e.g., by 'budding' from the highest-latex-yielding trees on to 'stocks' of very hardy but lower-yielding types).

In order to illustrate the vicissitudes – on the financial front – of the rubber-growing industry, the following figures provide eloquent testimony.

Throughout 1922 its average price per lb (London) was $9\frac{1}{2}$d and during 1925 it was 25d; and at one period during 1932 it fell to $2\frac{1}{8}$d! Price movements from 1964 onwards are summarized for this product on the page facing Sir Roy Harrod's Preface.

Similar illustrations might be given in respect of wool and other fibrous basics as well as for all the non-ferrous metals; and in fact for practically every other type of raw material.

H.6 ANOTHER QUESTION AS TO INITIAL INDEX. If the supply of Commodity 'Y' had been such as to cause market prices as at date of PSC's inception to have fallen by (say) 50 per cent below the preceding quinquennial average of its costs – assuming this to have been taken as the level of the *initial* Index for 'Y', – would not the level of its *initial* low *point* be such as to force market prices up to (or above) that level and thereby encourage excess production for an obviously artificial market?

Reply: Admittedly such a situation might arise if the statutory implementation of this system was invariably based on the formula which (*solely for illustration*) is set down in paragraph B.2 et seq. But, of course, any such state of affairs as that hypothesized would have been 'catered for' by an appropriate proviso in some such terms as the following (always assuming that it was decided that the *initial* Index was normally to be related to – if not at *par* with – the immediately preceding quinquennial average cost, cif):

> If the average of costs of any eligible commodity had declined over the (say) 36 months immediately preceding date of PSC's inception to a level that was below the quinquennial average of such costs by a (stated) percentage, the *initial* Index for that commodity *shall be related to that preceding triennial* average, and NOT to the higher *quinquennial* average.
>
> Moreover, in any such case, the volume of a BLOCK (of such product) shall be equivalent to only (say) 5 per cent of the volume imported during the preceding twelve months, and NOT the equivalent of 10 per cent of the annual average over the preceding quinquennium; thereby 'hastening' the downward adjustments of its Index and *points* in the event of PSC's being required to make extensive purchases of that commodity.

What needs appreciation is that there are very many ways in which the functioning of this system can be geared (as emphasized in B.24). What is vitally necessary, however, is that once the initial gearing had been determined and publicized, it could not be altered excepting by Statute to have effect only after a prescribed period of notice (as in B.24).

H.7 A BRITISH PSC'S INFLUENCE ON WORLD PRICES. As the UK's imports of commodities – although considerable – represent only a small proportion of total annual world outputs, is it tenable to suggest that a British PSC's functioning could actually stabilize *world* prices for any commodity?

Reply: Perhaps one illustration may suffice. The average annual world mine-production of copper from 1965 to 1969 (incl.) was some six million tons* of which the UK's annual

---

*In 1972 it was estimated at 7 million tons.

imports were rather more than 500,000 tons – about $8\frac{1}{2}$ per cent of world output of virgin copper.

One cannot foresee at what level the *initial* copper Index would be set; but, for convenient illustration (and perhaps not unrealistically) assume that this was set at £500 per ton – with an *initial* low *point* (Index minus 10 per cent) at £450, and an initial (conditional) HIGH *point* (Index plus 10 per cent) at £550.

Next assume that, in due course, PSC took into reserve (at the behest of sellers) say 20,000 tons. The probability is that most of this would be on *deposit* (see B.14) at *no investment cost to PSC*. But, if PSC had to *buy* the whole 20,000 tons at £450 per ton, its then total investment outlay would be £9 million. Thereafter, for as long as any part of such reserve copper was so held, the *market price* in the UK for any substantial purchase of this metal would be most unlikely to rise above the then *effective* HIGH *point* of £550 per ton – at which PSC would sell on demand. Moreover, in such circumstances, no copper-using industrialist *in any part of the world* (unless coerced by an import tax *imposed by his own Government*) would be disposed to pay more for copper than its cost at PSC's HIGH *point – plus relevant freight charges*.

However, this would not mean that he would in fact need to buy from PSC: rather would it mean that he would be hardly likely to pay more for copper (as a market price) domestically or anywhere else than its cost if bought from PSC; and copper sellers (competing as such) would make the best bargain they could (B.15) within the then limits of the effective copper 'band', i.e., between £450 and £550 per ton. Thus it would seem that the holding by PSC of a mere 0.33 per cent (or less) of the world's annual average mine-output of copper could stabilize the price of this metal in all parts of the world – freight costs apart. Manifestly, in the event of a persisting real world shortage (as distinct from an artificial or temporary shortage) prices inevitably rise, exhausting the reserves held by a British (and any other) PSC.

If, in the event, a British PSC had to pay for a first full copper BLOCK (which, with the preceding annual average of the UK's imports of this metal at – say – 500,000 tons, would be 50,000 tons) the *investment* involved would total £22$\frac{1}{2}$ million. In the event the cost (cif) of UK's copper imports (of 466,000 tons) in 1973 at £302 million exceeded that in the immediately preceding year (of 442,000 tons) at £191 million by £101 million. What the corresponding figures will be for 1974 remains to be seen!

If PSC were required to buy in *excess* of a first BLOCK, its payments could be deferred for three years (B.10); and, at the intake of *each* additional BLOCK (if any) the copper Index and *points* would automatically fall in value by 5 per cent of their *initial* levels (B.6).

Copper, a highly important essential commodity, is a wasting asset. It would therefore seem extremely unlikely that other copper-importing nations (or their nationals) would sit back and 'allow' a British PSC to accumulate immense reserves of a metal that could be bought from that PSC only at a premium of 22.2 per cent above what that Corporation had itself paid. What needs emphasis is that once substantial reserves had been established (by *any* nation's PSC) market prices would be held within known limits (B.13 (b)).

H.8 RANGE OF EFFECTIVE 'PRICE BAND'. Would a 'price band' equivalent to 22.2 per cent of the low *point* be a sufficient margin to provide for lucrative operations by intermediaries – brokers and dealers?

Reply: The margin of 22.2 per cent is purely illustrative. It could be that the enacting legislation might result in a wider or (possibly but not probably) narrower margin. Thus, if it were decided that the *points* should be 12 per cent below and above an *initial* Index of (say) £100 per ton, they would become: low *point* £88; and (conditional) HIGH *point* £112 – with a cash margin of £24 between PSC's buying and (conditional) selling prices; and £24 is 27.27 per cent of a low *point* at £88. It is not with such relatively minor details that this book is concerned. Its sole objective is fully to explain the principles on which the proposed system is based – a pattern of readily predictable cause and effect.

In Conclusion

While I have been writing this book there has developed an atmosphere of gloom throughout the Western World – not least within the United Kingdom. From time to time there have been tiresome forebodings as to the possible breakdown of Government – and, *in Britain*! even the emotive word 'revolution' has been used – with talk of building up what sections of the media have termed 'private armies' or the like. All this must surely add up to absurdity.

Nevertheless it is admitted on all sides that we are inevitably in for a (comparatively) tough time over the next year or two – and maybe for longer. But that need be over only a relatively short term if we exercise that commonsense which is one of the most widely shared attributes of the British. At worst the people of Britain would be infinitely better off than during the Second World War, because the most dismal possible prospect could mean no more than shortages of certain essential foods and clothing. If such a situation should arise it could be met by fixation of prices of necessities in short supply – inevitably accompanied by rationing. Of course it would be a novel – though not necessarily harmful – experience for the younger generation (the under-forties) to have to savour a modicum of the past tribulations of their elders; 'modicum' is used because in peacetime it would be *only* rationing that we should have to endure – happily unaccompanied by the horrors of the blitzes plus the heart-rending results of conflicts in the actual fighting zones. And we should survive. But it is certainly not here suggested that any such measures are more than remote possibilities.

Among the many bewildering features of the situation in late 1974 has been the conflicting nature of reports as to harvest prospects in the major grain producing countries. We were led to expect that there would be bountiful harvests in North America, Australia, France and Britain – and in Russia. Then came unfavourable weather conditions with disconcerting predictions as to the extent

145

to which yields could be successfully garnered. These sorts of occurrences are not new. They will happen again – and so will seasons in which generous yields will be harvested to fill granaries once more to over-flowing – as recorded in Genesis. Let the prudence of Joseph whose foresight was vindicated be revitalized via the system once again advocated in this work.

It is now fifty years since, in a book I wrote in 1924, I first commenced to advocate the establishment of reserves – specifically of wheat. An introduction to that work* by the then Prime Minister (later Earl Baldwin of Bewdley) contained the following passage: 'The economic facts set down in his text may have more far-reaching consequences than the author contemplates.' But nothing came of that.

Since then, as mentioned in Chapter 1, I have continued writing on the same theme with each of my books being lauded in the responsible Press and in parliamentary debates. My writings are not those of an academic economist but of one who has had personal experience of the problems of the producer of basic needs; as well as from the standpoint of the consumer. And by consumer one means not only the now generally well-fed, well-clothed people whom one sees on all sides in Britain and the rest of Europe, in North America, Australasia and among those of European stock in other parts of the world. One has in mind mankind as a whole; and those who have seen the plights of the undernourished in India, Africa and South America will the better understand one's outlook.

While this book is being printed the United Nations World Food Conference will be deliberating in Rome. As an Editorial in *The Times* (28/10/74) commented, 'It is not hyperbole to say, in the terms of one of the preparatory documents for the conference, that ". . . a prodigious effort for the mobilization of resources, physical, financial and human, is called for – an effort based on the realization that human society is indeed confronting one of the most crucial problems that has ever occurred in its long history" '.

But with every possible good intention what is that Conference likely to achieve? Can there be a harnessing of co-ordinated international effort? One earnestly hopes there can be, but it is indeed difficult to see how proposals that could lead to a more equitable order can be actually implemented by international administration via the United Nations – *dis*united as that Organization is in so many respects. One has only to look through the terms of any

*Colloquially styled *The Kangaroo Keeps on Talking*.

International Commodity Agreement to see the complexities involved in futile efforts to adjust supply to demand in respect of any single commodity – as witness what is in the preceding chapter.

For my own part I cannot begin to wrestle with any problem unless and until I can reduce it to terms of kindergarten. And that is what I have sought to do in devising the system I advocate and which is surely innately simple. The whole problem hinges upon the value of money in terms of essential goods and services (and vice versa) – as emphasized at the outset of this work. Let the producer be given assurances that his output will have minimum value and that, irrespective of effective commercial demand at or above that minimum level, the whole of his (then) 'excess' production can be transformed into reciprocal buying power. He will then put forward his best efforts. Moreover, with that assurance he will be able to secure safely invested capital (and here the International Bank for Reconstruction and Development could surely fulfil its purpose) to facilitate and increase production with no possibility of market collapse without notice sufficiently long for the producer to adjust his particular type of enterprise. Admittedly in some cases such readjustments could present difficulties, but these would be relatively minor.

In conclusion, perhaps I may be excused for quoting the peroration of an address entitled *Post-War Reconstruction Based on Price Stabilization* which I gave to a largely attended meeting of the Institute of Export in London in April 1941:

. . . It will lie within our power to put the economy of the world to rights so that no longer shall poverty stalk in the midst of plenty in this or in any other country; so that no longer shall unemployment, malnutrition and their attendant social evils shackle the progress of civilization. There is no visible limit to the world's wealth – or to its ordered and balanced production and distribution; nor is there to human industry and enterprise; and there is assuredly no visible limit to the material requirements of men. The way lies open to us to initiate and to implement the means of ensuring that, in due course, the basic wealth of the world shall be placed and maintained at the disposal of all nations, of all peoples, on the same terms.

And, as victors [it will be conceded I was an optimist at that crucial period] in this great war for religious, personal, social and political freedom, it would be fitting that we, the British peoples, should put the more material affairs of men in that state of good order which is so long overdue. Thereby would sound political and economic policy march hand-in-hand with good morality.

With the advent of 1975 I sense no reason to alter that statement by one iota.

Biographical Note

Leo St Clare Grondona, Australian born of English-Irish parentage*, after leaving Xavier College in Melbourne, spent three years on a million-acre sheep and cattle station in Queensland – by turn drover, stockrider and junior overseer; and occasional tutor to children remote from schools. His *Adventures of a Jackeroo* appeared when he was nineteen. Returning to Victoria he engaged in a wide range of farming enterprises. He served with the Australians in World War I when he was so severely wounded as to preclude his resuming work on the land. He joined the Federal Department of Repatriation and was soon in charge of that Department in NSW. He was with the Australian Delegation to the Imperial Economic Conference in London in 1923 following which he became Director of Information at the Australian section of the British Empire Exhibition. He wrote *The Romantic Story of Australia* (to which his Prime Minister, later Viscount Bruce of Melbourne, contributed a Preface) and followed this with *The Kangaroo Keeps on Talking* (to which the then British Prime Minister – later Earl Baldwin of Bewdley – wrote an Introduction).

His *Empire Stocktaking* (1930) was accorded eulogistic leading article and reviews; and two years later he produced *Britons in Partnership* of which *The Times* said: 'This is a drastic project for the reclamation of the vast estates of Empire – a door to realities which cannot be read without a glow of exhilaration.'

Late in 1934, he was appointed District Commissioner in the Special Areas in NW England. When the Chief Commissioner, Sir Malcolm Stewart, resigned in 1938, Mr Grondona did likewise and

*The author's father was Charles Henry Grondona, an Englishman (whose forebears had been Italian) who went to Australia in 1885. He was active in promoting the Federation of the six (then) Colonies, as a representative of Victoria at the preliminary Conferences which led to the establishment of the Commonwealth of Australia in 1901. He died shortly afterwards when only forty-three.

149

became economics consultant to Intercement, SA, in Paris. In early 1939 his *National Reserves for Safety and Stabilization* appeared. While this, too, was enthusiastically received by the responsible Press, the imminence of war put paid to its then consideration by HM Government. Its author joined the British Army in 1940. He was commandant of one of the chief prisoner-of-war interrogation centres. Some recollections of his experiences in regard to Marshal Messe (GOC Italian Forces in North Africa), F.M. von Rundsted, F.M. von Thoma and other high-ranking Germans, as published recently in the *Royal United Services Journal*, attracted widespread interest.

On the termination of hostilities in Europe, he became commandant of the Political Instructional Centre for German prisoners – several thousand of whom volunteered to attend series of courses conducted on university lines, under Foreign Office auspices, until August 1948.

In 1958, he produced *Utilizing World Abundance* – a post-war elaboration of *National Reserves* – which was likewise commended in the Press, as well as by MPs of all Parties in debates in the Commons.

In early 1960, he was invited to Australia to present a thesis on his stabilizing system at the XIIth International Congress of Scientific Management in Melbourne – where twenty-nine nations were represented. His Parliamentarian friends suggested that he visit, also, several other Commonwealth countries, and to facilitate his reception at Ministerial levels, letters were sent in advance by the Chairman of the Conservative Commonwealth Affairs Committee (now Lord Mortenmere) and by Mr Harold Wilson – then Shadow Chancellor of the Exchequer.

In the event, Mr Grondona had long discussions with Finance Ministers in Rawalpindi, New Delhi, Kuala Lumpur, Singapore, Canberra, Wellington (NZ) and Ottawa; and he addressed many groups of Parliamentarians in those capitals. Great interest was evinced in his proposal in all these countries, but none was in a position to implement it; because his system can be effective only if administered by a great commodity-*importing* nation – as distinct from countries that are primarily *exporters* of basic commodities.

When re-visiting his native land, he travelled widely as a guest of the several States, and later produced *Australia in the 1960s* to which the then Australian Prime Minister, Sir Robert Menzies, wrote an appreciative Preface.

Biographical

It may be apposite to conclude these notes with a quotation from a sentence from *The Times Review of Industry* in its comments on that book: 'Mr Grondona's writings about Australia and the Commonwealth over the past thirty years have won for him an enduring place in the respect and affection of his fellow countrymen.'

That observation was perhaps as gratifying to Mr Grondona as it was to those of his friends who saw it.

EDWARD HOLLOWAY
Honorary Secretary
Economic Research Council

Acknowledgements

The encouragement afforded me over many years by Sir John Reiss, BEM, Chairman of the Associated Portland Cement Companies Limited, is warmly appreciated.

I have been constantly stimulated by the interest of Sir Roy Harrod, Professor Lord Kaldor, Lord Roberthall and Donald Tyerman – as expressed in their prefaces. I am grateful, too, for the co-operation of the several Organizations concerned with the International Commodity Agreements mentioned in Chapter 7: Mr Ernest Jones-Parry and Miss R. M. Baines, OBE, in respect of the International, and the Commonwealth Sugar Agreements respectively, Mr Jean-Henri Parotte, Mr H. W. Allen, Mr J. A. N. Wallis, and Mr H.-J. Pritze respectively in regard to the International Agreements concerned with Wheat, Tin, Coffee and Cocoa.

My contact with these Organizations has been greatly facilitated by the help of Lorraine Simons and Stephen Leach, B.SC.

Finally, I wish to express my gratitude to my secretary Elizabeth Gray whose patience and outstanding efficiency have been of inestimable value.

6 Knightsbridge Court,   L. ST C. G.
Sloane Street, London SW1

Index

References are to headed sections in the individual chapters, except where specified as page numbers (p. 9, etc.).

Index

Index

Index